SERIES EDITOR:
**John Andrews**

**Len Quigg**

**Pauline Wylie**

# GCSE
## ENGLISH for CCEA
# REVISION BOOK

analyse

evaluate

timing

revise

technique

checklist

practice

advice

## Hodder Murray

A MEMBER OF THE HODDER HEADLINE GROUP

*Rewarding Learning*

# CONTENTS

## Paper 2 Section A: Writing 44

## Paper 2 Section B: Reading 48

## Checklists! 85

# Introduction

Let's start by making the situation clear – the purpose of this text is not to try to equip you with the basic skills required to be able to tackle CCEA GCSE English (that groundwork is covered in **GCSE English for CCEA**). This book is designed to assist you as a soon-to-be CCEA GCSE English candidate to hone the skills that you have already acquired so that you can maximise your level of performance in the examination. Understanding the specific demands of each question and the appropriate style of response will allow you to answer effectively.

Targeting of the answer has to be matched by your ability to work within strict time limits. This is all too often overlooked in the hurly-burly of revision. It is not enough to be aware of *what* has to be done and *how* it has to be done, you have to complete it in the allotted time! It is vital that you involve yourself in timed practice sessions – this is sensible preparation!

This book analyses all the available question types and explains exactly what the examiner expects from you. There are sample answers with supporting commentary to explain the strengths and shortcomings of these answers.

This book contains a concluding section, 'Checklists'. Here, for each of the practice tasks, there is a checklist of the points that are likely to form the basis for an answer. These will give you the opportunity to check up on the quality and relevance of your own responses and see exactly where your answering has been appropriate and what else might have been included.

Understanding the exact demands of an exam and being properly prepared to meet them is the best way to deal with those pre-exams nerves.

# How the book is organised

This text is structured in the same order as the examination that you will be sitting. The various practical revision sessions that it offers are categorised by paper number, question number and revision session.

This means, for example, that in **Practical Session 1.2.4** the '1' refers to Paper 1; the '2' means it targets the second question, and the '4' indicates that it is the fourth task on that particular question.

## Tiers of entry, details of the examinations and the nature of the assessment

| | Tier of entry | Available grades |
|---|---|---|
| **GCSE ENGLISH** | Foundation | C–G |
| | Higher | A*–D (E may also be awarded) |

| Paper | Time allocation and elements of the exam |
|---|---|
| **PAPER 1: two sections** | Section A: One hour<br>Testing: Reading comprehension based on literary prose<br>Number of questions: Three |
| | Section B: One hour<br>Testing: Writing to review, analyse and comment<br>Number of questions: One (essay) |
| **PAPER 2: two sections** | Section A: One hour<br>Testing: Writing to inform, explain and describe<br>Number of questions: One (essay *or* letter *or* article *or* speech) |
| | Section B: One hour<br>Testing: Reading non-fiction and media texts<br>Number of questions: Three |

## Assessment

The Assessment Objectives have not been included in this text. It is perhaps more important that you are aware of the broad principles that are used to assess the various sections of the exam.

A form of positive assessment is used. In other words you will be credited for what you *have* achieved, rather than what you have failed to do!

Any errors in spelling, grammar and punctuation will **not** be taken into consideration whilst assessing the Reading sections of these exams. However, when Writing is being assessed, these mistakes will be of significance. For those of you who have problems with writing accurately, consider tackling the Writing sections first in each of the exams.

# Managing your time

The position of this section at the beginning of the book should make its importance clear. Proper time management will allow you to maximise your exam performance.

You have probably spent more than a year at school or college developing the skills required for GCSE English. It is critically important that you can make use of these skills within the time frame imposed by the examination. Know exactly how much time to spend on each question and how to use that allotted time most effectively. Practising working within these time frames is crucial if you are to be successful!

Know how much you are capable of writing in 8, 10, 15 and 45 minutes. These are the sorts of time slots into which the exam breaks down. Below is sound advice about how you should be making use of your time in the examinations – detailed, question-specific advice is included in the relevant sections.

# Paper 1

## Section A: 3 questions

You will only have between 10 and 20 minutes in each case to answer the three questions. Don't waste ANY of this time – it would, however, be a big mistake not to spend roughly one quarter of that time planning and preparing each response.

## Section B: 1 question

You have 60 minutes to answer this question. Aim to write *a minimum of two sides*. It is critical that you take 10 or 15 minutes to think about this question, in order to develop and effectively plan your response. It is **not** a matter of writing about each of the prompts and then finishing off with your own view on the matter!

Feel free to use a page of your answer booklet to develop a quick plan – just cross it out afterwards. Rough work is not assessed – don't waste time on unnecessary detail or worrying about neatness!

Remember – trying to write too much can be as damaging as writing too little!

# Paper 2

## Section A: 1 question

You have the same time allocation as the writing task in Paper 1 (60 minutes). Again, take 10 or 15 minutes to think about this question and plan your answer. Mould your writing style to suit the form and the audience. Think – plan – write!

## Section B: 3 questions

As with Section A of Paper 1, you will only have between 10 and 20 minutes in each case for the three questions. Spend some minutes planning and preparing each response.

# Paper 1 Section A: Reading

There will be three questions on this section of the paper:

- the 'setting' question (could be either Question 1 or 2)
- the 'character study' question (could be either Question 1 or 2)
- the 'writer's craft' question (always Question 3).

For revision purposes, here, we will begin by looking at the 'setting' question.

# Question 1: The 'setting' question

Setting has an important part to play in all stories. It is one of the means by which a writer will engage the reader. It works by:

- rooting a story in a specific place and time
- helping the reader picture scenes the writer chooses to focus on
- evoking a particular mood/atmosphere – e.g. fear, tension, joy or sadness
- preparing the reader for what might happen and so creating a sense of anticipation.

This question in the GCSE English examination will test your understanding of how a writer has employed setting in a specific section of the comprehension passage.

Let's look at a typical question 1:

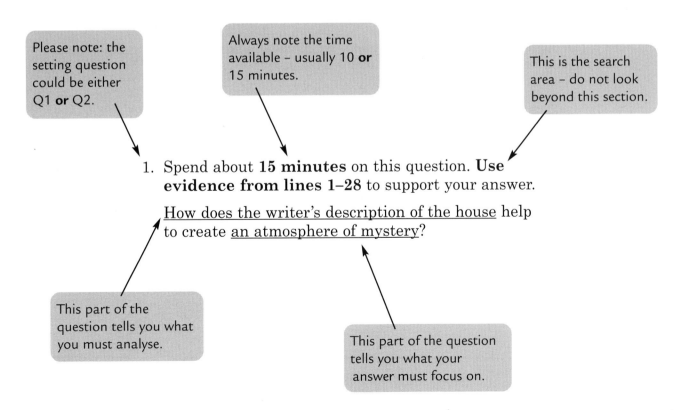

Please note: the setting question could be either Q1 **or** Q2.

Always note the time available – usually 10 **or** 15 minutes.

This is the search area – do not look beyond this section.

1. Spend about **15 minutes** on this question. **Use evidence from lines 1–28** to support your answer.

   How does the writer's description of the house help to create an atmosphere of mystery?

This part of the question tells you what you must analyse.

This part of the question tells you what your answer must focus on.

# Using your time most effectively

**Planning your answer:**

- re-read the question – make sure you understand the main focus
- note the search area and re-read the relevant section
- your exam paper is for you to use so feel free to underline/highlight useful material
- make *brief* notes (on the exam paper if you want) of the points you are going to make and any relevant writer's devices you have noticed.

**Writing your answer:**

- use your notes as a basis for your answer
- take a new paragraph for *each* new point
- if it helps, remember to PEE in each paragraph – make a POINT, give the EVIDENCE to support this point and EXPLAIN what effect the writer intended.

# Time to get practical!

## Setting: Rooting a story in a specific place and time

A writer will often begin a novel or short story by establishing a sense of the location where the events of the story are to unfold. How this is presented to the reader is crucial, as the impression created will influence the reader's reactions and emotions.

## Practical session 1.1.1

**Here is the opening to a novel. Read it and then consider what impression of the place is being conveyed and how this is achieved.**

You don't walk through Thorne Edge by yourself after dark. Not unless you're wrong in your head you don't. It's one of those great, sprawling estates they shoved up in the fifties to solve the housing shortage. They shoved it up so fast on the hillside north of Barfax they forgot about shops and pubs and cinemas, so if you live on Thorne Edge you have to go down town to find something to do. The sense of isolation this causes, together with the general squalor of the place, has turned some Thorne Edge residents mean. Even coppers only go in twos.

It's a funny place, Barfax. When they were building Thorne Edge it was a wool town: hulking great mills and thousands of little black houses crammed together in the valley, smoking like hell. Mucky Barfax they called it, and it was. There were people in Barfax who'd never had a lungful of clean air in their lives. You'd see them in the early mornings, coughing and hawking at bus stops.

> Mucky Barfax. Where's there's muck, there's brass, they used to say. There was too. People used to come from all over to work in the mills of Barfax. So many came that the town started to spread up the surrounding hillsides. Estates sprang up: red brick semis and concrete roads and patches of raw, yellow clay they called gardens. Thorne Edge was one of them.
>
> It's not like that now in Barfax. The mills have shut and they've knocked a lot of them down. A lot of the people have gone away and most of the others live out in the estates. Where the houses were, there's supermarkets and warehouses and little glass office blocks, most of them empty. There's just the lamp factory now, Ambler's, where they make light bulbs and fluorescent tubes and stuff. That's where most people work. There's a big new hotel and a shopping centre and that's about it. A few pubs. They've turned some of the pubs into wine-bars.
>
> From *Staying Up* by Robert Swindells

This opening tells us a number of things about the setting:

*The impression created is of an awful place that is wearing down its residents –*

☛ the blunt and direct opening two sentences are a warning about Thorne Edge
☛ even the names, Thorne Edge and Barfax, sound harsh and unappealing
☛ bleak phrases are used to describe the nature of Thorne Edge: 'The sense of isolation ... the general squalor'
☛ the place, with no facilities, has soured the residents – they are 'mean'
☛ the estate's toughness is such that 'Even coppers only go in twos.'
☛ the place is not only bleak, it is unhealthy and repulsive: 'thousands of little black houses crammed together'/'never had a lungful of clean air in their lives ... coughing and hawking at the bus stops.'
☛ the history of the town's rise is outlined – a place that expanded unpleasantly: 'Estates sprang up: red brick semis and concrete roads and patches of raw, yellow clay they called gardens'
☛ economic decline has set in: 'It's not like that now ... The mills have shut ...'
☛ even the few developments that have taken place fail to lift the feeling of gloom: 'There's a big new hotel and a shopping centre and that's about it.'

## Setting: Helping the reader picture a scene

Good writing pulls the reader into the midst of what is happening. To achieve this, a writer will use details to help the reader 'see' particular scenes. Presenting a scene in this way fulfils a number of purposes. It helps:

- to make writing more vivid and interesting
- the reader to empathise with a character and to become involved in the situation
- to establish a particular mood/atmosphere (more of this in the next section).

# Practical session 1.1.2

**Consider the two examples that follow:**

- **How have details been used to help the reader picture each scene being described?**

- **What purposes do you think each of the writers has attempted to achieve? (Look again at the three bullet points at the bottom of page 3.)**

## Example one:

I darted through the broken fence and into the garden of Ballindoon House. The garden was full of broken glass, tin cans and old prams, partly hidden by a jungle of tall weeds. The walls of the house were covered in ivy and the dark empty windows looked gloomy ...

When I was inside I wasn't exactly scared, even though I didn't feel like laughing. It was pretty weird. The windows were boarded over and it was very dark. Most of the floorboards were rotten and it was a tricky job to avoid falling down one of the many holes. There was a smell like old cupboards, and a creaking noise that might have been caused by me treading on the broken boards – or by rats; a nasty thought when you hadn't anything to throw at them ...

So, treading carefully, I made my way out of the basement and up the rickety stairs to the ground floor. I found myself in a big squarish hall but I couldn't make out many details because very little light came through the boarded up windows. From the hall a door led into what was, I supposed, the front room. I pushed it open and went in. The door swung to behind me, closing with a little bang. The room was empty except for some rubbish in one corner, great pieces of wallpaper hanging from the walls and a huge fireplace which looked as though it might fall down at any moment.

From 'The Haunting' by Mary Fitzgerald

## Example two:

'God knows, Jim, is there ever going to be an end to this weather?' remarked Dermot Duffy, the fireman, to his companion, Jimmy Gleeson.

'It's a dirty night to be heading for Cork right enough,' agreed Jimmy as the pair of them strolled along the platform towards the locomotive that hissed quietly at the head of the Cork train.

It was a dirty night. The dim lamps of the station yard beyond the platform were shrouded in steam but the falling rain was still visible in these patches of light. The rain belt that had been over the country for the past three days still showed no sign of lifting. The station was quiet, even for a Friday night, and those few passengers heading south would have no trouble finding seats on the train ...

The glowing heat from the firebox was welcome as the two men set about preparing for the journey. Dermot began stoking the fire while Jimmy cast his eye over the gauges in the smoky cab, checking steam pressure, brake pressures and water temperatures. Gazing across the bleak rain-soaked station yard with its network of tracks glistening through the darkness, Jimmy wished he was home in Inchicore, his feet up before the fire, listening to the wireless or doing the crossword in the evening paper.

From 'Night Train' by Nuala Lavin

See **Checklists!** on page 85 for a list of possible points.

# Setting: Creating a particular mood/atmosphere

First of all, look at this very short example:

> The hedgerow was beaded with silver. In the fog the leaves dripped with a deadly intensity, as if each falling drop were a drop of acid.
>
> From 'A Red-letter Day' by Elizabeth Taylor

You could make the following comments on how the writer is beginning to build up an atmosphere full of threat and imminent danger:

- ☛ the first sentence describes a familiar scene: dew drops in a hedge. There is a sense of delicate beauty in 'beaded with silver'. It is as if the writer is describing a piece of jewellery
- ☛ the writer's choice of language in the second sentence, however, introduces an element of menace into the scene. This is clearly conveyed in the phrase 'dripped with a deadly intensity'. The alliteration here reinforces the impression of malice
- ☛ the repetition of the word 'drop' imitates the rhythm of the drips as they fall from the leaves
- ☛ ominously, acid is a dangerous, toxic substance – not something we would normally associate with such a scene.

# Practical session 1.1.3

Now, consider the two following examples in the same way.

**What mood is being conveyed in each case and how has this been achieved?**

## Example one:

> The exam was held in the art room of the Grammar School. The walls were hung with plaster casts of tigers' mouths and human lips, utterly silent and utterly threatening. As I left the room at the end of the afternoon, even the air through which I walked seemed to crumble in ruin.
>
> From 'The Examination Result' by Alun Williams

## Example two:

> The sun was not yet up, and the lawn was speckled with daisies that were fast asleep. There was dew everywhere. The grass below my window, the hedge around it, the rusty paling wire beyond that and the big outer field were each touched with a delicate, wandering mist. And the leaves and the trees were bathed in the mist, and the trees looked unreal, like trees in a dream. Around the forget-me-nots that sprouted out of the side of the hedge were haloes of water. Water that glistened like silver. It was quiet, it was perfectly still. There was smoke rising from the blue mountain in the distance. It would be a hot day.
>
> From 'The Country Girls' by Edna O'Brien

See **Checklists!** on page 85 for a list of possible points.

## Practical session 1.1.4

This next passage is followed by a sample answer along with helpful tips on how to answer a setting question – it will also make clear what you should not do!

Try writing your own response to the question before reading the answer.

**How does the setting in this extract add to the sense of unease?**

Ralph swung the car onto a byroad ... Within a mile, verges began to intrude, and moss to grow between the tyres. Hedgerows closed above the car. Ralph throttled back, his eyes hunting for a farm gateway in which to turn. But the only houses were ruinous tumbles of ivied crumbling walls and tumbled thatch, entrances closed by stone walls or barbed wire. He drove until the surface all but gave out and the hedges were brushing the car ...

He stopped adjacent to a rusty gate and got out. Here wasn't such a bad place to explore. He'd spend an hour or so just walking and thinking. It was a pleasant day: cold, but crisp and bracing after the stuffy heat of the car ...

He grabbed the top bar of the gate and braced himself to vault across, but thought better of it. He wasn't such a young man any more and the gate felt ready to fall. Lank yellow grass, killed by autumn frost, drooped across it, and the bottom bar, where it rested on the ground, was fretted with rust. He climbed cautiously across and set off uphill towards a rocky knoll covered by brush and scrubby trees ...

The scrubby wood grew on a limestone crag, an ancient reef on which the teething seas had gnawed long before dinosaurs were born. Useless for farming, it had been left in a primeval state ... with threadbare patches of stunted blackthorn and the occasional hawthorn or larger tree growing where it could. It seemed not to have been touched by the hand, or even the foot, of man ... and goats, or perhaps deer, had stripped the bark from many trees, activity that had resulted in small clearings here and there, with some skeletal limbs still standing ...

Then it struck him that this must be Carrigaphookha: the Rock of the Pooka, or devil. Ralph hadn't heard the legend behind the name but he could guess – there were hundreds of such legends all over rural Ireland. If he felt anything at being in so sinisterly named a place, it was a momentary and delicious thrill.

It was indeed a thrilling place! ... Rocks were everywhere: slippery polished outcrops underfoot; thickly mossed boulders piled on each other in sometimes fanciful shapes in the twig-filtered watery sunlight; treacherously flagged pavements, mossy and bare, split and tilted by tree roots. Some yellow leaves hung limply from the hazels and dropped to the ground as he brushed the branches; a few red berries that had escaped the birds and beasts dangled from rowans and hawthorns; here and there the brilliant russet of a crispy beech stood out. The dull brown of bark and withered bracken, spattered with dead briar leaves, bright as arterial blood, and the dark moss and purple blackthorns, formed a background. The effect, with the sun now sinking, was an odd, sombre cheerfulness ... a few yards back into the brush all was silent as – yes, the grave. He shivered with that delicious thrill.

Even the birds were silent ... once or twice, a magpie or starling chattered narkily at his approach, or a pigeon noisily broke cover and flapped frantically away, causing his heart to thump ...

He looked at his watch. It was then that apprehension hit him. It was after four o'clock. Where had the time gone? ... His apprehensiveness was heightened when he realised than in an hour or less it would be dark.

From 'Horns of a Whimsical Eden' by Michael Carragher

# Sample answer

An opportunity is missed here as there is no attempt to comment on how this helps to create a sense of unease.

Some examples selected for valid comment on how the writer's opening begins to create unease. description.

> The writer is describing somewhere derelict, empty and broken down. We are told about how the 'verges began to intrude'. This suggests that Ralph is beginning to feel enclosed and claustrophobic. This creates an uneasy feeling. The fact that the 'hedges were brushing the car' increases the sense that Ralph shouldn't be in this place.

> We see that there are 'crumbling walls' and 'tumbled thatch' in sight. It is now obvious that this place has been abandoned for years.

> The writer also tells the reader that entrances were 'closed by stone walls or barbed wire'. This suggests that this may be a dangerous area or that trespassers are not wanted. Barbed wire also reminds us of prisons and places where visitors are not welcome. There is also the impression that somebody is hiding something.

A relevant comment that offers a valid interpretation of the writer's intentions.

This point would have been strengthened by offering an analysis of a range of the words and phrases associated with death in this passage.

> The writer uses phrases like 'killed by autumn frost'. This is a very cold phrase. We as readers are being made to think that something is going to happen as the word 'killed' is used.

> The tension increases when 'skeletal limbs' are mentioned. The story also mentions blood, briar leaves which are 'as bright as arterial blood' and dark moss. We also learn that the place is called Carrigaphookha.

These are all apt references but there is no attempt to link these to the question.

This is simply re-telling of the story. Do not fall into this trap.

> Near the end of the passage, Ralph is startled by the noise of a pigeon flapping frantically away, causing his heart to thump. He then looks at his watch and realises that it is after four o'clock. He wonders where the time has gone. He realises that it will soon be dark.

> All these things add tension to the passage and create an uneasy atmosphere. The writer very clearly describes a spooky scene. Also, at first, Ralph isn't scared but by the end he is starting to panic as he realises he is all alone in a scary place.

A general summary, although the final sentence does recognise Ralph's change of mood.

## A summary of the answer:

This had the potential to be a much better answer. The candidate demonstrated some sound understanding about how a sense of unease was achieved through the setting. Unfortunately, however, there was not a sustained focus on the question as he/she drifted into telling the story and didn't explore or support some points fully.

This next section offers you a series of passages to work through. In each case read through the passage carefully, twice, and then allow yourself *no more than 15 minutes* to write your response. Evaluate your answer by comparing it with the appropriate checklist at the back of the book. Learn from this and move on to the next example when you're ready.

## Practical session 1.1.5

### How does the setting help to convey the anxiety felt by the character?

The gate, hidden behind the yews and laurels, had not been opened for a long while. The wood was damp and swollen and slimy with lichen. It caught on the untrimmed grass as she pushed it back and it hung open behind her as she stepped out onto an overgrown path which appeared to lead into an area of woodland. Pushing her hands down into her pockets she walked cautiously forward ...

Somewhere near her a pheasant crashed out of the undergrowth with an explosion of alarm calls and she stopped, her heart thundering under her ribs, staring round. As the frightened bird flew low through the trees and out of sight the silence returned. Even the cheerful rustling of the leaves overhead died away as the wind dropped. She stared round, straining her ears for some kind of sound.

... She gazed at the trees for a moment, strangely reluctant to walk any further, the hairs on the back of her neck prickling as she became aware suddenly that eyes were watching her from the thicket on her left. Holding her breath she turned her head.

For several seconds she and the fox stared at each other, then he was gone. He made no sound but the space he had filled beneath the old hawthorn bush was empty. She was so relieved she almost laughed out loud. Whatever thoughts had raced through her head at that moment they had not included a fox.

With a lighter heart she stepped forward, aware that the wind was once more blowing strongly in her face and two minutes later she rounded the corner near the holly bushes to find herself on the edge of an overgrown lawn. In front of her stood the house.

It was an old, grey building with gabled roofs and mullioned windows, the plastered walls covered in ivy and wisteria and scarlet Virginia Creeper. She stood quite still, staring. Belheddon Hall. Her birthplace.

Almost on tiptoe she crept forward. Internal shutters gave the windows which faced her a strangely blind aspect, but for a moment she had the strangest feeling that she was being watched from somewhere behind those shutters.

From *House of Echoes* by Barbara Erskine

See **Checklists!** on page 85 for a list of possible points.

# Practical session 1.1.6

**How does the writer convey to the reader the unpleasant nature of sleeping rough?**

If you think sleeping rough's just a matter of finding a dry spot where the fuzz won't move you on and getting your head down, you're wrong. Not your fault of course – if you've never tried it you've no way of knowing what it's like, so what I thought I'd do was sort of talk you through a typical night ...

So you pick your spot. Wherever it is (unless you're in a squat or a derelict house or something) it's going to have a floor of stone, tile, concrete or brick. In other words it's going to be hard and cold. It might be a bit cramped, too – shop doorways often are. And remember, if it's winter you're going to be half frozen before you even start. Anyway you've got your place, and if you're lucky enough to have a sleeping-bag, you unroll it and get in.

Settled for the night? Well maybe, maybe not ... You could be peed on by a drunk or a dog. Happens all the time – one man's bedroom is another man's lavatory. You might be spotted by a gang of lager louts on the lookout for someone to maim. That happens all the time too, and if they get carried away you can end up dead. There are the guys who like young boys, who think because you're a dosser you'll do anything for dosh, and there's the psycho who'll knife you for your pack.

So, you lie listening. You bet you do. Footsteps. Voices. Breathing, even. Doesn't help you sleep.

Then there's your bruises. What bruises? Try lying on a stone floor for half an hour. Just half an hour. You can choose any position you fancy, and you can change position as often as you like. You won't find it comfy, I can tell you. You won't sleep unless you're dead drunk or zonked on downers. And if you are, and do, you're going to wake up with bruises on hips, shoulders, elbows, ankles and knees – especially if you're a bit thin from not eating properly. And if you do that six hours a night for six nights you'll feel like you fell out of a train. Try sleeping on concrete then.

And don't forget the cold. If you've ever tried dropping off to sleep with cold feet, even in bed, you'll know it's impossible. You've got to warm up those feet, or lie awake. And in January, in a doorway, in wet trainers, it can be quite a struggle. And if you manage it, chances are you'll need to get up for a pee, and then it starts all over again ...

So. You lie on your bruises, listening. Trying to warm your feet. You curl up on your side and your hip hurts, so you stretch out on your back so your feet stay cold and the concrete hurts your heels. You force yourself to lie still for a bit, thinking that'll help you drop off, but it doesn't. Your pack feels like a rock under your head and your nose is cold. You wonder what time it is. Can you stop listening now, or could someone still come? Distant chimes. You strain your ears, counting. One o'clock? It can't be only one o'clock surely? I've been here hours. Did I miss a chime?

What's that? Sounds like breathing. Heavy breathing, as in maniac. Lie still. Quiet. Maybe he won't see you. Listen. Is he still there? Silence now. Creeping up, perhaps. No. Relax. Jeez, my feet are cold.

A thought out of nowhere – my old room at home. My little bed. What I wouldn't give for – no, mustn't. Mustn't think about that. No sleep that way. Somebody could be asleep in that room right now. Warm and dry. Safe. Lucky sod ...

And so it goes on, hour after hour. Now and then you doze a bit, but only a bit. You're so cold, so frightened and it hurts so much that you end up praying for morning even though you're dog-tired – even though tomorrow is certain to be every bit as grim as yesterday.

From *Stone Cold* by Robert Swindells

See **Checklists!** on page 85 for a list of possible points.

# Question 2: The 'character study' question

This will usually be the second of the three questions you will be set on the prose fiction passage. It tests your understanding of a particular character presented by the writer.

Let's look at a typical question 2:

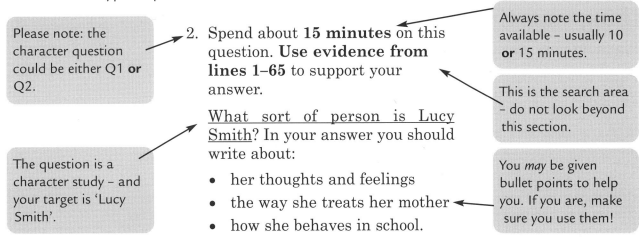

Please note: the character question could be either Q1 **or** Q2.

2. Spend about **15 minutes** on this question. **Use evidence from lines 1–65** to support your answer.

   <u>What sort of person is Lucy Smith</u>? In your answer you should write about:

   - her thoughts and feelings
   - the way she treats her mother
   - how she behaves in school.

Always note the time available – usually 10 **or** 15 minutes.

This is the search area – do not look beyond this section.

The question is a character study – and your target is 'Lucy Smith'.

You *may* be given bullet points to help you. If you are, make sure you use them!

The question requires you to study how a person is presented in the passage and identify clearly in your answer the **main features** of his/her 'character' or personality.

Remember that to score highly in this question, you need to do more than just report what the writer says about the character. You need to delve more deeply into the character and show what he/she is really like. You have to 'read between the lines' and recognise **what is implied or suggested** about the character.

## Some handy hints!

You can identify what characters are like by studying some of the following:
- what they look like
- what they do
- what they say (and how they say it)
- their thoughts and feelings
- what other people say about them
- how other people treat them or react to them
- how the writer influences our attitudes towards them, for example through the language or images used to present them.

# Types of question

In CCEA English Paper 1 Section A, there are *two* main types of question used to test your understanding of a character in a piece of fiction:

1  straightforward **analysis** of the character
2  the **empathy** approach, which requires a more imaginative response.

We will deal with these separately.

# 1 Analysis of a character

In this type of question, you study the person closely, identify the main features of his/her character and explain these clearly and convincingly. The most common forms of this type of question are: *What do you learn about Andrew Jones?* or *What sort of person is Lucy Smith?*

## Using your time most effectively

### Planning your answer:

- get a clear grasp of the outline of the story and an understanding of the situation and the characters

- re-read the relevant section, searching for points/clues/suggestions about that particular character

- jot your points/comments down, perhaps in the margin of the exam paper, to help you develop your answer

- find as many points as you can. Your study of the character should be as thorough as possible and you must display as much understanding of him/her as you can, **within the set time limit**. Find at least five or six points, proving that you have a broader understanding of the complexity of the character

- remember that you need to justify each point you make; that means you must prove that your point is valid by referring to evidence in the passage. Brief and clearly supportive quotations, in inverted commas, help. For example:

  *Jane's almost painful shyness in the presence of strangers is shown by her 'constantly downcast eyes' and the way she blushes 'all too readily'.*

### Writing your answer:

- put together the points you have identified in your notes into a coherent answer which presents a clear and accurate analysis of the character.

## Time to get practical!

In the first passage, some key points about the central character are identified for you. Try to spot some other points yourself.

## Practical session 1.2.1

In this extract, set in Ireland in the 1940s, a farmer has just returned home from market.

> The man reined in the horse beside the gate and stepped onto the road. He approached the two women leisurely, pulling a pipe and a plug of tobacco from the bib pocket of his dungarees. The women waited for him.
>
> The man set the empty pipe between his teeth and blew through it a few times. He put his hand inside one bulging jacket pocket, and worked out a blood-stained corded package wrapped in butcher paper. He handed it to the younger woman. The woman took the meat without a word. He brought another package from the other pocket.

'Sausages. For the childer [*children*].' He handed that over too. 'You might set the pan a-squealing, woman. I had a long day of it on the fairgreen [*market square*].'

Bridie took a step towards the laneway ...

The man began to whittle at his plug. He was a big man, up on six foot, stout and heavy, with shoulders as square as a door. He might be forty-five, he might be more, though not a grey rib showed in the hair beneath his grubby cap. His black moustache was bristling, and covered his upper lip completely. Stubble several days old grew on his cheeks and throat, so densely that the porter stains down the seams that framed his chin could hardly be seen against it.

His sister glanced at him, but didn't speak ... The wife was behind them, silent.

The man shredded the tobacco between his palms, blew through his pipe once more, and took it from his mouth.

'Da?'

'Aye, Tom?'

'Do you want me to take the mare up?'

'Do that, son. Heel the cart up fornenst [*in front of*] the stable door, and put them in there for the time being. Go handy, now.'

From 'Women and Men' by Michael Carragher

Concentrate on the following 'handy hints':

* what he looks like
* what he does
* how other people react to him.

You could make the following comments about him:

☞ he is a big man and his powerful strength is suggested in the simile 'shoulders as square as a door'

☞ he is careless about his appearance – he has a 'grubby cap', 'porter stains' in his beard and 'stubble several days old'

☞ he is arrogant – he 'leisurely' prepares his pipe – the others have to wait for him

☞ he is a dominant character, seen in the way he instructs the 'woman' to fry the sausages

☞ there is an air of threat about him, as both women seem afraid to speak to him. They meekly accept his orders. (Can you see any other evidence in the passage to support this view of him?)

☞ he seems to be kind to his children. He has brought sausages from the market as a treat for them; he also speaks kindly to his son Tom at the end of the passage.

## You have a go!

Try the next two passages. In each case, spend no more than 15 minutes answering the question. The first passage is followed by a sample answer along with some helpful comments – these will also be useful in making clear what you should not to do!

If you tackle the question yourself first, you can compare your answer with the specimen answer.

## Practical session 1.2.2

**What do you learn about Uncle Joe? In your answer you should consider:**

- **his niece's thoughts about him**
- **the comments his wife (Aunty Eileen) makes about him.**

In this passage the writer recalls her Uncle Joe.

When I was in my early teens I used to spend my holidays with Aunty Eileen and Uncle Joe, who lived in a high terraced house near Donaghadee …

At that time my Uncle Joe was a tall and very bony-looking man in his forties. He would sometimes shave at the kitchen mirror, his braces dangling loose as he concentrated mightily on each stroke with a cut-throat razor. I was fascinated by the hollows behind his collar bones. They were so deep that they looked spooky to me. The boniest part of him was his round bald skull, which came out in freckles if he got the sun.

Uncle Joe suffered from a curious thing called hypochondria. Until I was thirteen or so I though this was a kind of snake but as far as I know it doesn't occur among animals at all. It affects some grown-ups. They think they're ill when they're not. My Uncle Joe was the first hypochondriac I ever knew.

In the beginning I believed him when he said there was something the matter with him because I didn't know any better, and a man who can come out with hair-raising words like aneurisms, duodenums, ducts and bile seemed to know what he was talking about.

One day, as we brushed the lino on the stairs, I asked Aunty Eileen if Uncle Joe really *was* sick. She made a sharp little 'tch, tch' sound with her tongue, then whisked me into their bedroom on the middle floor. Opening a drawer lined with wallpaper, she showed me a selection of Uncle Joe's medicines – boxes of pills, liquids in coloured bottles, tubes of ointment and one or two fearful gadgets. The drawer gave off an odour of Wintergreen, or some such rub for sore backs. 'There you are,' said Aunty Eileen. 'He takes some of this stuff every blessed day in life! I don't know, it's like a chemist's shop.'

'But what exactly is the matter with him, Aunty Eileen?' I asked.

'Everything, love. You name it, he's got it.'

'Well, he doesn't look sick,' I said. 'Just a bit thin.'

'Don't I know rightly, that's the whole point! It's all in his head, dear.'

We finished brushing the middle flight of stairs. Aunty Eileen flicked a small pile of dust on to a card I was holding, and after a glance down the hall, began to speak quietly.

'Listen, don't let him worry you with his talk. Your Uncle Joe tried to join the army when the war started but the army wouldn't have him. It was the medical, you see, they said something inside him was murmuring. Well, the shock *that* gave him started him on pills and he's been taking them ever since like sweets.'

'And *was* there something murmuring inside him?'

'Oh I dare say. Nerves, probably.' She giggled and pinched my cheek and told me to pay no attention to him. 'Not to worry, pet. He's still in the land of the living.'

From 'The Electric Rejuvenator' by Sam McBratney

# Sample answer

One of Uncle Joe's habits is reported.

More relevant evidence is presented to show the extent of his hypochondria.

The background to the man's condition and his wife's view of it, are suitably highlighted by the candidate.

The candidate begins appropriately by summarising the details of the character's physical appearance.

The central feature of the character is described and the final sentence points towards the character's pre-occupation with his condition.

> *From this passage we do learn quite a lot about Uncle Joe. We are told of his physical appearance. In his forties, he is a tall and bony man with a round bald skull that comes out in freckles if he gets the sun. According to the narrator, he had spookily deep hollows behind his collar bones.*
>
> *We are told that he would sometimes shave at the kitchen mirror with his braces dangling as he concentrated on shaving.*
>
> *Uncle Joe is a hypochondriac. His niece didn't initially understand the full implications of the term and thought at first that he was unwell. This was in part due to her Uncle's use of complicated medical terms like 'aneurisms'. This demonstrates the extent of Uncle Joe's fixation with his 'condition'.*
>
> *In the third paragraph we are shown the extent of Uncle Joe's hypochondria when Aunty Eileen shows the girl 'a selection of Uncle Joe's medicines'. We are told by his wife that he takes some of this stuff every day.*
>
> *The last paragraph sheds some light on Uncle Joe's past. His hypochondria had its origins in a failed medical during the war. The shock of it 'started him on pills' and he has eaten them 'like sweets' ever since. His wife's giggling makes it clear that she doesn't think his 'murmuring' is anything to be worried about – 'He's still in the land of the living'.*

## A summary of the answer:

This is a competent answer to a straightforward question. You will notice that there are few conclusions or inferences to be drawn about the character; however the candidate sticks to the task of drawing together all the relevant material into the answer.

## Practical session 1.2.3

**What do you learn about Bridgie Thomas?**
**(Do not just focus on what the person looks like and how she behaves,**
**but also on: what other characters say or think about her and what the**
**writer wants us to think about her, revealed through the vivid**
**comparisons she uses to describe her.)**

Here, an eccentric old lady, Bridgie Thomas, is presented through the eyes of
three young children.

On the twelfth exhausted, rackety bong of the town clock, Mrs Tudge and Lally Tudge came
waddling around the corner in a shimmer of striped heat ... The bell rang over the door of the
Penny Bazaar as they squeezed through the doorway.

Bridgie Thomas followed behind the Tudges. Bridgie Thomas lived in Sebastopol Terrace in a
house filled with boxes of sacred old bones, and scrapbooks that contained the yellowing
toenails of long-dead saints.

She was a thin, poker-legged old woman. She kept her head bent low as she walked and the
pleats of her long shiny grey skirt were hot blades in the heat.

She was a maniac, but not a dangerous one, as far as they knew.

She wore a huge black crucifix around her neck, it was big enough to hang on a church wall.
The weight of lugging it around had curled her bony back into a grey, darned, woollen hump.
Under her clothes they said she wore vests that she knitted from stinging nettles and thistles.
She put tin-tacks in her shoes to please God.

She had quick darting eyes the colour of boiled goosegogs [*gooseberries*]. Hairs grew from her
sharp, pointy chin, as white and wispy as spring onion roots.

She was in the wrong part of town. Usually she only walked from her house in Sebastopol Terrace
to the Catholic church and back; once a fortnight to the Co-op for brown bread and prunes.

They watched her through eyes narrowed against the bright, hot light. She carried a Fyffes
banana box that she set down very carefully in front of the town clock. From a pocket of her
skirt she took a pair of black thick-lensed spectacles and put them on. They magnified her eyes:
huge, green and mad.

She stepped up on top of the rickety box, and swayed dangerously. But didn't fall off.

Pity.

The crucifix swung across her chest like a giant pendulum ...

'What's she doing?' Iffy asked.

'She's going to make a speech by the look of it,' said Bessie.

'Who to? There's nobody here, only us,' Fatty said. Bridgie cleared her throat and thrust her
hairy chin skywards. Her neck was as wrinkled as a dead tortoise.

'Hark unto me. I call upon the people of this town, I, the handmaid of Christ. I come to warn
you. For I tell you that God the Father is sorely tried by your ungodliness. He is sending a
warning to the sinners of this valley ...'

'She's bloody crackers,' Fatty said, screwing a grubby finger into the side of his head.

From *A Jarful of Angels* by Babs Horton

See **Checklists!** on page 86 for a list of possible points.

# 2 The 'empathy' approach

The answer to this type of question requires a very different style from the straightforward 'character analysis' response. Empathy is the ability to use your imagination to sense what it is like to be another person, in a given situation.

In this question you will be told to '*Imagine you are Andrew Smith. Present his thoughts and feelings about ...*'

You may be given some bullet point ideas to help you organise your answer. If so, make good use of these; they will help you develop an effective and relevant answer.

This style of question gives you the opportunity to range more widely in your answer, but make sure that **anything you include is suggested in the passage**. You should not introduce material that is not in the original passage.

In the empathy question, you have to demonstrate your understanding of the specified character by actually **'becoming'** him/her. You have to adopt the persona of one of the people in the story. In order to answer this question effectively you need to have a clear grasp of the character whose viewpoint you are asked to present.

The examiner will ask you to use one of the following forms: a **diary entry** or a **letter to a close friend or relative**. Your answer should present the character's feelings in an open, honest and appropriate way. Your answer will be judged on how convincingly you have presented the thoughts and feelings typical of that character.

## Planning your answer:

- you need a clear grasp of the situation the character is in
- jot down comments or highlight material that will help you develop your answer
- remember you should reflect the personality of the character, present thoughts and feelings that are typical of him/her
- reflect the mood of the character in his/her situation, through use of tone
- present an appropriate attitude towards other characters in the story.

## Writing your answer:

- remember to use **the first person ('I')** to present the character's personal feelings
- put together the points you have identified in your notes into a coherent answer which presents a clear picture of the character
- use the sort of language that the character would use in the situation described.

# Time to get practical!

In the first passage, some key points about the central character are identified for you. Try to spot some other points yourself. This is a diary entry in which the writer, 'confiding' in his diary, reveals to us some aspects of his rather curious personality!

## Practical session 1.2.4

Adrian Mole would like to be a poet – in this extract he goes on a trip to the Lake District to see if being in the area where the great poet William Wordsworth (writer of the poem 'Daffodils') once lived will inspire him.

> Woke up at 6am in the morning ...
>
> After measuring my chest and shoulders I had a thorough wash in cold water. I read somewhere ... that 'cold water makes a man of you'. I've been a bit worried about my maleness lately, somewhere along the line I seem to have picked up too many female hormones.
>
> I've been to see the doctor about it, but as usual he was most unsympathetic. I asked if I could have some of my female hormones taken out. Dr Grey laughed a horrible, bitter laugh and gave his usual advice, which was to go out and have my head kicked about in a rugby scrum. As I was leaving his surgery he said, 'And I don't want to see you back here for at least two months.' I asked, 'Even if I'm taken seriously ill?' He muttered, '*Especially* if you're taken seriously ill.' I'm considering reporting him to his superiors; all this worry has affected my poetry output. I used to be able to turn out at least four poems an hour, but now I'm down to three a week. If I'm not careful I'll dry up altogether.
>
> In my desperation I went to the Lake District on the train. I was struck down by the beauty of the place, although saddened to find that there were no daffodils flashing in my outer eye as in William Wordsworth the old Lake poet. I asked an ancient country yokel why there were no daffodils about. He said, 'It's July, lad.' I repeated loudly and clearly, (because he was obviously a halfwit) 'Yes, I know that, but why are there no *daffodils* about?' 'It's July,' he roared. At that point I left the poor deranged soul. It's sad that nothing can be done for such pathetic geriatric cases. I blame the government. Since they put rat poison in the water supply most of the adult population have gone barmy ...

> I walked around the lake trying to feel inspired, but by tea-time nothing had happened so I put my pen and exercise book back into my carrier-bag and hurried back to the station to catch the train back to the Midlands.
>
> It was just my luck to have to share a compartment with hyperactive two-year-old twins and their worn-out mother. When the twins weren't having spectacular tantrums on the floor they were both standing six inches away from me, *staring* at me with unblinking evil eyes.
>
> From *True Confessions of Adrian Albert Mole* by Sue Townsend

This amusing diary entry tells us a number of things about Adrian:

- ☛ he would like to be seen as strong, tough and masculine. Each morning, he measures his chest and shoulders!
- ☛ he is concerned about his health, seen in the frequent visits to his long-suffering doctor!
- ☛ he is intolerant in his attitude towards others, seen in his dismissal of the old man he meets as a 'yokel' and a 'halfwit'
- ☛ he is very naïve (you might say stupid!) in not realising that daffodils bloom in the early spring, not in July. His description of the old man as a 'halfwit' hilariously underlines his own stupidity!
- ☛ he has a tendency to exaggerate things: the 'ancient yokel's' supposedly stupid answer to his question proves that 'most of the adult population have gone barmy'
- ☛ he is again foolishly naïve in thinking that poetic inspiration can be turned on at will
- ☛ he is self-conscious and easily embarrassed, as seen in his reaction to the 'hyperactive twins' on his return journey
- ☛ an important point about Adrian is that he takes himself much too seriously, something which we can see from his revelations in the diary entry. Adrian, however, is totally unaware of this flaw in his character.

When *you* write your answer to an empathy question, you must try to present an understanding of the character whose persona you have adopted.

## Time to get practical!

Try writing empathy-type responses based on the following two passages. In each case, spend no longer than **15 minutes** on your answer. **Practical session 1.2.5** gives some ideas to help you write the answer, followed by a sample answer with a useful commentary. Try **Practical session 1.2.6** unaided.

## Practical session 1.2.5

Here a young man called Stanley is brought to a tough prison camp.

> The guard led Stanley to a small building. A sign on front said YOU ARE ENTERING CAMP GREEN LAKE JUVENILE CORRECTION FACILITY.
>
> The guard led Stanley into the building, where he felt the welcome relief of air-conditioning.
>
> A man was sitting with his feet up on a desk. He turned his head when Stanley and the guard entered, but otherwise didn't move. Even though he was inside, he wore sunglasses and a cowboy hat. He also held a can of soda, and the sight of it made Stanley even more aware of his own thirst.

He waited while the bus guard gave the man some papers to sign … Then the man in the cowboy hat walked around the desk to Stanley. 'My name is Mr Sir,' he said. 'Whenever you speak to me you must call me by my name, is that clear?'

Stanley hesitated. 'Uh, yes, Mr Sir,' he said, though he couldn't imagine that was really the man's name.

'You're not in the Girl Scouts anymore,' Mr Sir said.

Stanley had to remove his clothes in front of Mr Sir, who made sure he wasn't hiding anything. He was then given two sets of clothes and a towel. Each set consisted of a long-sleeve orange jumpsuit, an orange T-shirt, and yellow socks …

Mr Sir told him he should wear one set to work in and one set for relaxation. Laundry was done every three days. On that day his work clothes would be washed. Then the other set would become his work clothes, and he would get clean clothes to wear while resting.

'You are to dig one hole each day, including Saturdays and Sundays. Each hole must be five feet deep, and five feet across in every direction. Your shovel is your measuring stick. Breakfast is served at 4.30.'

Stanley must have looked surprised, because Mr Sir went on to explain that they started early to avoid the hottest part of the day. 'No-one is going to baby-sit you,' he added. 'The longer it takes you to dig, the longer you will be out in the sun. If you dig up anything interesting, you are to report it to me or any other counsellor. When you finish, the rest of the day is yours.'

Stanley nodded to show he understood.

'This isn't a Girl Scout camp,' said Mr Sir.

…Then he led Stanley outside into the blazing heat.

'Take a good look around you,' Mr Sir said. 'What do you see?'

Stanley looked across the vast wasteland. The air seemed thick with heat and dirt. 'Not much,' he said, then hastily added, 'Mr Sir.'

Mr Sir laughed. 'You see any guard towers?'

'No.'

'How about an electric fence?'

'No, Mr Sir.'

'There's no fence at all, is there?'

'No, Mr Sir.'

'You want to run away?' Mr Sir asked him.

Stanley looked back at him, unsure what he meant.

'If you want to run away, go ahead, start running. I'm not going to stop you.'

Stanley didn't know what kind of game Mr Sir was playing.

'I see you're looking at my gun. Don't worry. I'm not going to shoot you.' He tapped his holster.

'This is for yellow-spotted lizards. I wouldn't waste a bullet on you.'

'I'm not going to run away,' Stanley said.

'Good thinking,' said Mr Sir. 'Nobody runs away from here. We don't need a fence. Know why? Because we've got the only water for a hundred miles. You want to run away? You'll be buzzard food in three days.'

Stanley could see some kids dressed in orange and carrying shovels dragging themselves towards the tents.

'You thirsty?' asked Mr Sir.

'Yes, Mr Sir,' Stanley said gratefully.

'Well, you better get used to it. You're going to be thirsty for the next eighteen months.'

From *Holes* by Louis Sachar

**Imagine you are Stanley. Write a diary entry describing your arrival at Camp Green Lake. You should present your thoughts and feelings about:**

- **Mr Sir**
- **the camp**
- **and anything else you think is relevant.**

In this story Stanley, understandably, does not say very much but we can imagine that a lot would be going on in his mind at this time. In his diary entry, therefore, you should allow those confused, frightened inner thoughts to pour out in an appropriate style.

With regard to Mr Sir, Stanley's thoughts and feelings might be based on some of the following features:

☛ menacing appearance – dark glasses/the gun
☛ sarcastic attitude – 'not in the Girl Scouts anymore'
☛ the precise instructions he gives about the work to be done
☛ desire to dominate – insistence on being addressed as 'Mr Sir'
☛ how he lets Stanley see the hopelessness of any possible escape
☛ cruelty in denying him a drink.

With regard to the camp, Stanley's thoughts and feelings might be based on some of the following details:

☛ the heat, and the consequent thirst
☛ the barren landscape
☛ the difficulty and monotony of the work
☛ the exhaustion of others – the kids 'dragging themselves towards the tents'
☛ the obvious brutality of the regime.

Stanley's tone in his diary entry will obviously reflect his fear and his desperation at the situation he has arrived in. You might begin the diary entry as follows:

> Today, I entered the world of the worst possible nightmare, Camp Green Lake. I just don't know how I'll survive here …

# Sample answer

This is a suitable and engaging opening that imaginatively captures Stanley's reaction to Green Lake.

A perceptive development of the detail of the story which demonstrates a real grasp of Mr Sir's treatment of the boy.

A series of appropriate statements and perceptive questions – a strong finish.

Notice how cleverly this information from the text has been included in the diary account.

This paragraph draws in some of the details from the story and sets them beside reactions that are appropriate – 'a nightmare'/ 'burning up'.

This is a competent final paragraph that pulls some of the stranger aspects of the story together.

> *Dear Diary,*
>
> *Today I arrived at what could only be described as a hellish prison camp – a desert version of Alcatraz. It's in the middle of nowhere, a lonely building called Green Lake – I couldn't understand the name because the one thing this place doesn't have for one hundred miles is water!*
>
> *The first person I met inside the refreshingly cool building wore sunglasses and a cowboy hat. I found that a little odd, but not as odd as his name – 'Mr Sir' I've to call him. I knew by the look of him that he wouldn't cut me any slack; 'You're not in the girl scouts anymore,' he told me, smirking. I reckon he was only drinking his soda to remind me how thirsty I really was – something I think I'm going to have to get used to!*
>
> *I had to remove my clothes in front of him, it was in case I was trying to smuggle something in, well, that's what he said. I was almost relieved to get into the weird orange and yellow overalls that are to be my uniform at Green Lake.*
>
> *The place sounds like a nightmare. Breakfast's at 4.30 am and it is followed by work. Mr Sir told me that they start at that time to avoid being out in the worst of the sun. It's awful, I've to dig one hole, five feet deep and five feet wide, every day! And I'll be out in that wasteland burning up in the sun until I've got it finished!*
>
> *I don't know if I can survive this. What's the point in digging these holes? And if I find anything interesting, I'm to report it – very strange. His gun, he informed me casually, was to shoot yellow-spotted lizards – what's that all about? I've a really bad feeling about this place!*

## A summary of the answer:

This is a competent answer that clearly demonstrates the candidate's understanding of the text. The strongest feature of the answer is the manner in which appropriate details have been developed to create a perceptive and convincing understanding of the boy's situation and very real concerns.

# Practical session 1.2.6

In this passage, set in America, the fourteen-year-old narrator is having problems with his big sister.

Saturday night, June 1956, now the sun going down at 7.50 pm and the sprinkler swishing in the front yard of our big green house on Green Street, big drops whapping the begonias and lilacs in front of the screened porch where Daddy and I lie reading. A beautiful lawn, new-mown, extends to our borders with the Stenstroms and the Andersons ...

I am taking it easy. Reclining on the porch swing, nestled in four pillows, a bottle of Nesbitt orange pop within easy reach. I am fourteen. In 1958 I will obtain my driver's license and in 1960 graduate from Lake Wobegon High School. In 1963 I can vote. In 1982 I'll be forty. In 1992, fifty. One day, a date that only God knows, I will perish from the earth and no longer be present for roll call, my mail will be returned, my library card cancelled, and some other family will occupy this house, this very porch, and not be aware that I ever existed, and if you told them, they wouldn't particularly care. Oh well, what can you do? I hope they appreciate the work I did on the lawn ...

And now out comes the older sister from the kitchen, all hot and bothered, and cries out, 'Why does he get to lie around and read books while everybody else has to do the work around here? I even had to do his laundry today – boy, talk about disgusting!' She makes a face. 'And he's supposed to dry the dishes and he just waltzes away and the pots and pans are sitting there in the dish rack!'

She stands over Daddy, hands on hips, her broad butt in the yellow Bermudas [*shorts*], her pale pimply piano legs. 'It takes two minutes to dry a few pots and pans, and he can't even be bothered to do that much!'

I explain to her the principle of evaporation, whereby the air absorbs moisture and objects such as pots and pans become dry in a short period of time with no need for human hands.

'Why do you have to be so stupid?'

I am only being reasonable, I explain.

She leans over Daddy and touches his shoulder, to bring him back to the point. 'Why do I have to do my chores and his too? It isn't fair!' You'd think she had spent ten years on a chain gang ...

Daddy says he wishes I would be kinder to my sister and do my share of the chores.

'I do the lawn.' And this is surely true. When the genius went away to the University I took over the lawn, which he, being a genius, had allowed to go to rack and ruin, and now take a look for yourself. Thick green turf. Dandelions vanquished ...

But the sister has Daddy wrapped around her little finger. She works him like a marionette [*puppet*]. She stands behind him, touching his shoulder, and he tells me to go dry the pots and pans. Even though I have mowed the entire lawn. 'I will,' I say. 'In a minute.'

'Why can't you do what you're told?' she hisses at me.

'Don't make a federal case out of everything.'

She looks daggers at me, poor ugly thing. A big shovel-faced girl with ... chubby thighs and cheesy hair and a very very bad personality. And that is the problem here, ladies and gentlemen. This is not about pots and pans. This is about a personality problem.

I am quite content here with my reading material, but this porky little whiner, Miss Misery, comes and ruins a perfectly lovely summer night, simply because someone knows enough about the scientific process of evaporation to let the pots and pans sit and dry by themselves instead of running in to dry them at her beck and call. This is the issue here.

'Go dry the pots and pans,' says Daddy. 'How many times do I have to tell you?'

'As soon as I move the sprinkler, I will go and put away the pots and pans, which are undoubtedly dry already.'

'So move it, then,' he says.

'I'll go check and see if it's ready to be moved.'...

'Not ready to be moved yet,' I say ...

The sister is not amused. She shakes her head and stomps into the house, her big yellow butt like two pigs fighting in a laundry bag.

From *Lake Wobegon Summer 1956* by Garrison Keillor

**Imagine you are the narrator's sister. Write a letter to your friend Judy, explaining to her all the problems you are having at home at the moment. In your answer you should present your thoughts and feelings about:**

- **your parents**
- **the work you have to do at home**
- **your horrible brother.**

It is obvious that the sister's tone in this letter will be one of jealousy, anger and frustration. She will have a number of not-too-pleasant things to say about her brother! Enjoy writing a suitably spiteful answer – but make sure you base it on the material in the passage!

See **Checklists!** on page 86 for a list of possible points.

# Question 3: The 'writer's craft' question

This is the question that carries most marks in this section. It is generally considered to be the most demanding, but there is no reason why you shouldn't tackle it successfully.

Let's look at a typical question 3:

> First information is about the available time – 20 mins.

> This is the key phrase to bear in mind when you're answering this question. Remember: **HOW**

3. Spend about **20 minutes** on this question. Use **evidence from the whole passage** to support your answer.

   How has the writer created a story that holds her reader's attention?

   In your answer write about:

   • the way in which the story is told from Alice's point of view

   • the use of words and phrases to develop the tension

   • how the story finishes.

> Next, comes the search area.

> The focus of the question has to be recognised and understood.

> Three bullet points for guidance – they are the areas you are to search in order to explain **HOW** the writer has held our attention.

## Using your time most effectively

### Planning your answer:

• re-read the instructions to see what part of the passage you are expected to use

• highlight the focus in the opening statement – for example, *engaging/exciting/humorous/frightening etc.*

• re-read the bullet points. Think how they relate to the focus – they will be the basis around which you should build your answer. They are guidance from the examiner as to what you should write about – they are your 'answer plan'

• for each bullet point, note down key words and phrases as you think of them – keep these to two or three words – enough to act as a trigger during the next 10–15 minutes

• go back and skim/scan the text, searching quickly for points you've overlooked or forgotten about – add any relevant items that you come across

• having assembled and noted your ideas, prioritise these and move on!

### Writing your answer:

• the number of points that you have to make will dictate the amount of detail that you can use – express yourself formally and concisely

- offer analysis of what the writer has done and back it up briefly with evidence

- keep the focus on the central issue in the question – *'Another thing that sustains attention is the writer's use of ...'*

- summarise incidents briefly; quote only individual words and phrases that you intend to comment on – put them inside 'inverted commas'

- for each new point take a new paragraph – it is a clear and simple method of flagging up that you've finished making one point and are moving on to the next

- work systematically through the bullet points and your 'notes' – don't re-tell the story.

# Time to get practical!

This next practical session is followed by an annotated sample answer – intended to help you see the 'dos and don'ts' of answering this type of question.

You can either write your own answer to this question *before* reading the annotated answer, or simply read the response and the commentary – whichever you think will be more useful for you.

## Practical session 1.3.1

Read the excerpt carefully; you then have **20 minutes** in which to answer the question.

> **How has the writer captured the attention of the reader with the opening to her story?**
>
> **In your answer consider:**
>
> - **the effect created by the use of the first-person narrator**
> - **the dramatic situation that unfolds**
> - **the use made of language.**

This passage is the opening to a book. Its setting is close to the trenches in the midst of the First World War.

BECAUSE I am an officer and a gentleman they have given me my notebooks, pen, ink and paper. So I write and wait. I am committed to no cause, I love no living person. The fact that I have no future except what you can count in hours doesn't seem to disturb me unduly. After all, the future whether here or there is equally unknown. So for the waiting days I have only the past to play about with. I can juggle with a series of possibly inaccurate memories, my own interpretation, for what it is worth, of events. There is no place for speculation or hope, or even dreams. Strangely enough I think I like it like that.

I have not communicated with either my father or mother. Time enough for others to do that when it is all over ... Why prolong the pain that they will inevitably feel? It may kill him, but then, like me, he may be better off dead. My heart doesn't bleed for her.

They are treating me with the respect apparently due to my class, and with a reserve due, I am sure, to the fear that I may be mad. How alarmed men are by the lurking demons of the mind!

Major Glendinning has not been near me, a blessing for which I am duly grateful. He will never make a man of me now, but I don't suppose he'll lose much sleep over that ...

By now the attack must be on. A hundred yards of mournful earth, a hill topped with a circle of trees, that at home would have belonged exclusively to the fairies, a farm, some roofless cottages, quiet unimportant places, now the centre of the world for tens of thousands of men. The end of the world for many, the heroes and the cowards, the masters and the slaves. It will no doubt be raining on them, a thick and evil February rain.

The padre comes to visit me from time to time. He showed me yesterday the gold cross he wears ... 'Have you Faith?' he asked me.

He didn't put it quite like that. He had a more sophisticated way of phrasing things, and also a certain embarrassment in asking what he made sound like an almost indecent question.

'I've never really thought about it.'

'Now is perhaps the time to think.'

I wished that he would go away. I was not, nor am I now, in the mood for soul wrestling, that is a pastime for those who have time to spare.

'It's a bit late now I fear, Padre. Faith is to comfort the living. It seems to me to be irrelevant for the dead.'

'You are alive.'

'Technically.'

'Comfort perhaps ...'

'I am comfortable, thank you. I ... I wonder always why you ... you know ... you ...' I put out my hand and touched his dog collar, 'well, representatives, seem to get such satisfaction in making us afraid of death. Be joyful in the Lord. Come before his presence with a song. That's not quite right, I know, but the drift is there. I shall sing gladly.

How many miles to Babylon? [*a children's nursery rhyme*]

Four score and ten, sir.

Will I get there by candlelight?

Yes and back again, sir ...'

I croak rather than sing. He held a hand up in distress.

'Your frivolity makes me uneasy.'

'I'm sorry. No need. We all must have our own way of dying.'

... He left soon after. I was sorry that I distressed him.

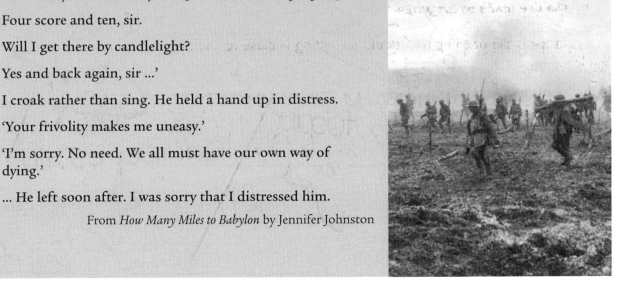

From *How Many Miles to Babylon* by Jennifer Johnston

See **Checklists!** on page 86 for a list of possible points.

# Sample answer

| | |
|---|---|
| Clear analysis of the style of narration – supported by an example. | *Everything that the army officer – our very personal narrator – is telling us about is negative and the fact that he doesn't care that he has no future gives the story a touch of sadness as well as making it intriguing – 'I am committed to no cause, I love no living person.'* |

More analysis of the central character's outlook and the effect the writer is creating.

*'... I have no future ... doesn't seem to disturb me unduly' gives us the impression that this man has a very unnatural way of thinking – all these things would disturb most people greatly. This only fuels the reader's curiosity.*

An analytical comment that touches on the narrator's view-point and the writer's use of language.

*He has a very individual way of looking at things as we see in his comments about 'the attack' – normally an unimportant place has 'now become the centre of the world for tens of thousands of men.' Again his challenge to the padre suggests someone who has his own very different outlook on life and death.*

An initially unsupported comment that is given some relevance by the next paragraph.

*His world has 'no hope or speculation for hope'; he is content that he'd 'be better off dead'.*

A reasonable point, the final phrase maintains the focus on the question.

*Obviously there is friction between the officer and Major Glendinning as implied in the comment 'He will never make a man of me now.' Again this helps to make us curious, therefore gaining our attention.*

More of the incidents of the story are analysed and tied into the question.

*The fact that the narrator sees no point in getting scared or upset about dying – as he discloses to the padre – is intriguing. We are surprised at the way he turns the tables on the clergyman, and interested by his singing of the child's nursery rhyme.*

A short paragraph that marks out the end of the response to the first two bullet points.

*All of the above help to draw the reader into this strange story – we want to know how this man's life has come to this very dramatic situation.*

A couple of perceptive observations are offered on the writer's use of language. Again both are supported by examples.

*Language is used to develop a sense of tension in the piece, 'It may kill him' or 'Faith is to comfort the living.'*

*Words are used in short, shocking bursts, for example, 'I love no living person.'*

## A summary of the answer:

There is a range of perceptive and supported points presented. The candidate initially considers the first bullet points together before commenting briefly on the use of language. This is a good, competent answer that keeps its focus firmly on the question.

The remainder of this section is given over to more passages and questions. They are intended to provide you with the opportunity for timed practice. In each case allow yourself 15 minutes to read the text and then 20 minutes to produce your answer. After you have completed your response, assess it against the appropriate checklist (p. 86).

Improvement will result from:

- tackling these questions in the systematic manner
- practising realistically by working 'flat-out' and keeping to the time limits
- learning from mistakes by analysing your performance with the help of the checklists that you will find at the back of the book.

# Practical session 1.3.2

**Why does the reader find this story engaging?**

**In your answer consider:**

- **the effectiveness of the writer's descriptions of the settings**
- **the way in which the story is told from the boy's point of view**
- **the build up of the suspense as the story comes to its conclusion.**

THE SUN was setting, spilling gold light on the low western hills of Rathlin Island. A small boy walked jauntily along a hoof-printed path that wriggled between the folds of these hills and opened out into a crater-like valley on the cliff-top. Presently he stopped as if remembering something, then suddenly he left the path, and began running up one of the hills. When he reached the top he was out of breath and stood watching streaks of light radiating from golden-edged clouds ... A short distance below him was the cow standing at the edge of a reedy lake. Colm ran down to meet her waving his stick in the air, and the wind rumbling in his ears made him give an exultant whoop which splashed upon the hills in a shower of echoed sound. A flock of gulls lying on the short grass near the lake rose up languidly, drifting like blown snowflakes over the rim of the cliff.

The lake faced west and was fed by a stream, the drainings of the semi-circling hills. One side was open to the winds from the sea and in winter a little outlet trickled over the cliffs making a black vein in their grey sides. The boy lifted stones and began throwing them into the lake, weaving web after web on its calm surface. Then he skimmed the water with flat stones, some of them jumping the surface and coming to rest on the other side. He was delighted with himself and after listening to his echoing shouts of delight he ran to fetch his cow. Gently he tapped her on the side and reluctantly she went towards the brown-mudded path that led out of the valley. The boy was about to throw a final stone into the lake when a bird flew low over his head, its neck a-strain, and its orange-coloured legs clear in the soft light. It was a wild duck. It circled the lake twice, thrice, coming lower each time and then with a nervous flapping of wings it skidded along the surface, its legs breaking the water into a series of silvery arcs. Its wings closed, it lit silently, gave a slight shiver, and began pecking indifferently at the water.

Colm, with dilated eyes, eagerly watched it making for the further end of the lake. It meandered between tall bulrushes, its body black and solid as stone against the greying water. Then, as if it had sunk, it was gone. The boy ran stealthily along the bank looking away from the lake, pretending indifference. When he came opposite to where he had last seen the bird he stopped and peered through the sighing reeds whose shadows streaked the water in a maze of black strokes. In front of him was a soddy islet guarded by the spears of sedge and separated from the bank by a narrow channel of water. The water wasn't too deep – he could wade across with care.

Rolling up his short trousers he began to wade, his arms outstretched, and his legs brown and stunted in the mountain water. As he drew near the islet, his feet sank in the cold mud and bubbles winked up at him. He went more carefully and nervously. Then one trouser fell and dipped into the water; the boy dropped his hands to roll it up, he unbalanced, made a splashing sound, and the bird arose with a squawk and whirred away over the cliffs. For a moment the boy stood frightened. Then he clambered on to the wet-soaked sod of land, which was spattered with sea gulls' feathers and bits of wind-blown rushes.

Into each hummock he looked, pulling back the long grass. At last he came on the nest, facing seawards. Two flat rocks dimpled the face of the water and between them was a neck of land matted with coarse grass containing the nest. It was untidily built of dried rushes, straw and feathers, and in it lay one solitary egg. Colm was delighted. He looked around and saw no one. The nest was his. He lifted the egg, smooth and green as the sky, with a faint tinge of yellow like the reflected light from a buttercup; and then he felt he had done wrong. He put it back. He knew he shouldn't have touched it and he wondered would the bird forsake the nest. A vague sadness stole over him and he felt in his heart he had sinned. Carefully smoothing out his footprints he hurriedly left the islet and ran after his cow. The sun had now set and the cold shiver of evening enveloped him, chilling his body and saddening his mind.

In the morning he was up and away to school. He took the grass rut that edged the road for it was softer on the bare feet. His house was the last on the western headland and after a mile or so he was joined by Paddy McFall; both boys, dressed in similar hand-knitted blue jerseys and grey trousers, carried home-made school bags. Colm was full of the nest and as soon as he joined his companion he said eagerly: 'Paddy, I've a nest – a wild duck's with one egg.'

'And how do you know it's a wild duck's?' asked Paddy slightly jealous.

'Sure I saw her with my own two eyes, her brown speckled back with a crow's patch on it, and her yellow legs ...'

'Where is it?' interrupted Paddy in a challenging tone.

'I'm not going to tell you, for you'd rob it!'

'Ach! I suppose it's a tame duck's you have or maybe an old gull's.'

Colm put out his tongue at him. 'A lot you know!' he said, 'for a gull's egg has spots and this one is greenish-white, for I had it in my hand.'

And then the words he didn't want to hear rushed from Paddy in a mocking chant, 'You had it in your hand! ... She'll forsake it! She'll forsake it! She'll forsake it!' he said, skipping along the road before him.

Colm felt as if he would choke or cry with vexation. His mind told him that Paddy was right, but somehow he couldn't give in to it and he replied: 'She'll not forsake it! She'll not! I know she'll not!'

But in school his faith wavered. Through the windows he could see moving sheets of rain – rain that dribbled down the panes filling his mind with thoughts of the lake creased and chilled by wind; the nest sodden and black with wetness; and the egg cold as a cave stone. He shivered from the thoughts and fidgeted with the inkwell cover, sliding it backwards and forwards mechanically. The mischievous look had gone from his eyes and the school day dragged on interminably. But at last they were out in the rain, Colm rushing home as fast as he could.

He was no time at all at his dinner of potatoes and salted fish until he was out in the valley, now smoky with drifts of slanting rain. Opposite the islet he entered the water. The wind was blowing into his face, rustling noisily the rushes heavy with the dust of rain. A moss-cheeper, swaying on a reed like a mouse, filled the air with light cries of loneliness.

The boy reached the islet, his heart thumping with excitement, wondering did the bird forsake. He went slowly, quietly, on to the strip of land that led to the nest. He rose on his toes, looking over the ledge to see if he could see her. And then every muscle tautened. She was on, her shoulders hunched up, and her bill lying on her breast as if she were asleep. Colm's heart hammered wildly in his ears. She hadn't forsaken. He was about to turn stealthily away. Something happened. The bird moved, her neck straightened, twitching nervously from side to side. The boy's head swam with lightness. He stood transfixed. The wild duck with a panicky flapping, rose heavily, and flew off towards the sea. ... A guilty silence chilled the boy ... He turned to go away, hesitated, and glanced back at the dark nest; it'd be no harm to have a look. Timidly he approached it, standing straight, and gazing over the edge. There in the nest lay two eggs. He drew in his breath with delight, splashed quickly from the island, and ran off whistling in the rain.

From 'The Wild Duck's Nest' by Michael McLaverty

See **Checklists!** on page 86 for a list of possible points.

The final revision element for Paper 1 Section A is the opportunity to tackle a complete section at either Foundation or Higher level. It is a chance to put together all the skills you've been practising into a realistic one-hour test.

## Practical session 1.3.3

# FOUNDATION TIER SAMPLE PAPER

### Paper 1: Section A

This section tests **reading** skills.

- Spend about **15 minutes reading** the passage carefully.

- Answer **all three** questions.

---

CHARLEY was six at the time, or maybe seven. His Mammie was beside him in a white apron, her hands on her lap doing nothing. His Daddy lay stretched in sleep on the sofa. Sunday evening was always quiet. The fire-glow filled the room. It glowed redly on Charley's knees and face, glinted on the fender, and threw shadows on the ceiling and the red-tiled floor. It was nice to be sitting alone with your Daddy and Mammie, feeling the heat on your knees, and listening to the kettle singing, and ashes falling in the grate. In the fire you could see animals and sometimes men and sometimes ships, and when your eyes got sticky you could just sit and look at nothing.

Suddenly the milkman knocked and Charley jumped. His Mammie went into the scullery for the white jug. His Daddy wakened and took out his big watch in the fire glow.

'Boys-o-boys!' he said. 'Is it that time?'

He got up and was on his feet when Mammie came back and placed the jug on the clean table. Daddy was very tall standing on the floor, with the fire winking on his watch-chain and his face all red and rosy.                                                                        14

'Do you think you'll go this evening?' Mammie said.

'Indeed I will,' said Daddy.

'Maybe you'd take Charley with you, he never gets anywhere.'

So Charley was going out with his Daddy, out at night when the lamps would be lit and all other wee boys in bed.                                                                              19

His mother put on his little round hat with the elastic that nipped him under the chin, and when he was going out the front door she stopped and kissed him.

'Say a prayer for your Mammie who has to stay at home,' she said.

And now they were walking down the street. He felt big to be out so late with the sky dark and the lamps lit. The snow had fallen. It wasn't deep snow, but it covered the ground, and lines of it lay on the black garden railings, and on the arms of the lamp-posts. The milkman's cart was near a lamp and its brass fittings shone and steam came from the horse's nose. The milkman said to his Daddy, 'A cold evening that,' and steam came from his mouth, too. Then his cans rattled. The cart moved on in front and the wheels began to unwind black ribbons on the snow.

They walked out of the street on to the road, on to the road where the trams ran. Charley put his hand in his Daddy's pocket and it was lovely and warm. Up in the sky it was black, as black as ink, and far away was the moon which Mammie called God's lamp, and stars were round it like little candle lights.

A tram passed, groaning up the hill where they were walking. Sparks, green ones and red ones and blue ones, crackled from the trolley, but the tram went on and slithered out of sight. And now there was nothing on the road only the snow and the black lines where the trams ran. Up above were the telephone wires covered with crumbs of snow, but the trolley wires were all dark. Presently they lit up with gold light and soon a black motor-car came slushing down the hill, covered with snow. Then it was very quiet.

Other people, big people all in black, were out and most of them were walking in the same direction as Charley and his Daddy. They passed shops, the sweetshop with Mrs. Dempsey standing at the door.

'Good-night, Mister Conor,' she said. His Daddy raised his hat, the hard hat that he wore on Sundays.

'Do you know Missus Dempsey, Daddy?'

'I do, son.'

'I know her; that's where I buy when I've pennies.' But his Daddy looked in front with the steam coming out of his mouth.

They passed policemen standing in doorways, stamping their feet, the policemen who chased you for playing football in the streets. But Charley wasn't afraid now, he was walking with his hand clutched tightly in his Daddy's – inside the big warm pocket.

After a while they came to the chapel. All the people seemed to be going to the chapel. It was dark outside, but a man stood in a lighted porch holding a wooden plate, and on the plate Charley's father put pennies.

Inside it was warm and bright. You could smell the heat as you walked up the aisle. His Daddy's boots squeaked and that was a sign they weren't paid for. They went into a seat up near the altar and his father knelt down with a white handkerchief spread under his knees. Charley sat with his legs swinging to and fro. At the sides were windows, and when tram-cars passed you could see lightning and blue diamonds and red diamonds.

Someone came in at the end of their seat and Charley and his Daddy had to move up. It wasn't nice for people to move you into a cold place, when you had the seat warmed.

A priest came out. Charley could answer the prayers like the rest and he felt very big. After a long time they stood up to sing and Charley turned round to look at the organ-man away high up at the back of the Church. The organ looked like big, hot-pipes. At the end of the hymn he said: 'Are we going home now, Daddy?'

'S-s-sh,' his Daddy said softly.

'Well, when are we going home?'

His Daddy didn't answer. Charley lifted the little round hat and began crackling the elastic and putting it in his mouth. His Daddy told him to sit at peace.

A priest came into the pulpit. He talked about lightning, and he said that the sun would be dark, and that the stars would fall from Heaven. He talked for a long, long time, but Charley fell asleep. After a while his father caught him by the arm and with difficulty he opened his eyes …

The organ began playing softly, very softly, and Charley turned to see what was wrong. A woman in the seat behind him was praying, her lips moving in a low whistle. He watched the moving lips and then they stopped suddenly. The woman was making a face at him and he turned and sat closer to his Daddy.

He filled his mind with everything, everything to tell his big brothers and sisters. There were boys with fat brass candlesticks and a priest with a golden cloak that sparkled with lights. God was on the altar, too, behind a little glass window with gold spikes all around it. A boy was shaking a silver thing like a lamp and smoke came out of it, nice smelling smoke, and if you shut your eyes it made a noise like nails in a tin.

The organ began to growl and people to sing. Charley put his fingers to the flaps of his ears. You could hear the noise very small, then it would get big like thunder, and if you moved your fingers in and out the noise would go ziz-zaz and a ah-aha-aaah! But it soon stopped. People bowed their heads and Daddy bowed his head too. Charley covered his eyes with his hands, but looked through his fingers to see what was going on. Someone coughed far, far away. Someone else coughed. Then it became so still you could hear your heart thumping.

The bell on the altar rang once. His Daddy whispered something to himself, and when the bell rang again Charley heard him say, 'My Lord and my God!' He thought of his Mammie and he told God to love his Mammie who had to stay at home. He closed his eyes and he saw her in a snowy apron, the white jug on the table and he wondered if she would have cake for his tea, cake with currants in it.

And now they were going home, out into the cold air, and on to the road where the trams ran.

His big brothers and sisters were in when he got home. They were taking tea and there was cake with currants in it on the table. They asked him questions, but laughed at his answers, so he just sat and ate his cake. But his Mammie was good and he told her that when the bell rang Daddy said, 'My Lord and my God!' But his Daddy didn't laugh at this. He just said, 'That child is dying with sleep, he should be in bed.'

So his Mammie brought him to bed, up to the bedroom ... He knelt and said his prayers on the cold, oilcloth floor. In bed it was cold, too, colder that the seat in the chapel. But it soon got warm; and he thought of the organ in his ears ... the tram that went up the hill with lights crackling from the trolley... and stars falling ... falling.

From 'Evening in Winter' by Michael McLaverty

1.  Spend about **10 minutes** on this question. Use evidence from lines 1–14 to answer the following question.

    How has the writer developed a sense of a cosy Sunday evening?

    [8 marks]

2.  Spend about **15 minutes** on this question. Use evidence from line 19 to the end of the passage to answer the following question.

    What sort of a boy is Charley?

    [10 marks]

3.  Spend about **20 minutes** on this question. Use evidence from the whole passage to answer this question.

    How has the writer created the convincing world of a young child?

    In your answer consider:

    *   the way the events of the story are seen from Charley's point of view

    *   the use of words and phrases

    *   the way the structure has been used to develop a child-like sense in the writing.

        [12 marks]

*See **Checklists!** on page 87 for a list of possible points.

## Practical session 1.3.4

# HIGHER TIER SAMPLE PAPER

## Paper 1: Section A

This section tests **reading** skills.

- Spend about **15 minutes reading** the passage carefully.

- Answer **all three** questions.

This is the opening from a science-fiction story.

How Jools Anton P'ntarr loved that girl from the Inner-Space Menagerie! Every time he saw her his heart beat on his ribs as if it wanted to be let out of its cage.

He watched her feeding a squit. The squit's green head lay flat on the water rather like a pretty lily – and here ended the resemblance to flowers. Perishing squits had teeth sharp enough to leave you counting up to ten with nine fingers. Then she checked the pressure in the tank inhabited by the hairy gloop from the planet Perseus. This was a heavy-gravity planet and poor hairy gloops exploded if the pressure dropped below a certain number. Pop! they went.

Not for the first time, Jools wondered what had made this wonderful person – who had such shape, intelligence and style – choose to work at the Inner-Space Menagerie. The college sent her here for two days a week as part of a work-experience course … she elected to come into this huge crystal hall, a place flooded with light, where the trustees had assembled a collection of life forms from the nearer planets. Ugly things, most of them, but their foul habits and vile perfumes were not enough to keep Jools away. He came here often to observe his beauty among the beasts.

And today was rather a special day, for he had resolved to approach her, and speak to her, and let her know that he existed. He stood beside the transparent pen where they kept the wheebler from the planet Dracena.

Oh beating heart be still! He spoke his first words to her. 'That's a very fine wheebler you've got there.'

'Yes, isn't it gorgeous,' she replied.

In all honesty Jools did not find it gorgeous. Frankly, the thing was revolting from all angles. The wheebler resembled a large lump of dough and possessed the power to deliver an electric shock of 1,000 volts. It could, besides, turn itself into virtually any shape or form, or even, when in the mood, turn itself inside out. Of all living things that Jools knew of, here was the one with the least sex appeal; and yet it remained one of the Inner-Space Menagerie's star attractions. **26**

'They begin life as a vegetable, you know,' she said.

'Yes, I can easily believe it,' said Jools.

'And they live for four hundred years. She's one of the miracles of the universe, aren't you, Dot?'

He wanted to tell her that she, too, was one of the miracles of the universe … Jools knew that he had been guilty of staring and cleared his throat for the little speech he had prepared in case the conversation hit an asteroid, so to speak.

'Perhaps I should say who I am. My name is Jools Anton P'ntarr and I'm in your compulsory ecology classes at college.'

'They're so boringly gross, aren't they?'

'Indeed they are …'

She looked at him out of two of nature's most perfect gems, both illuminated from within by her natural radiance; and he could feel himself melting. Oh bubbling blood, let him not get carried away and come out with a crass romantic utterance that would haunt him for days. He'd dreamed up thousands of these during compulsory ecology …

'Please tell me your name.'

'What do you want my name for? Pass me that bucket of liver.'

He passed the bucket of liver. 'So that I can say it to myself over and over again.'

'You definitely are missing a chromosome,' she observed. 'Who else do you know in college?'

'Perry Kepler. Bunny Goldman.'

'I know Bunny, he wears lovely clothes,' she said, opening a brute of a gate which said Authorized Personnel Only. The whooping primates had got wind of the liver by now and had taken to howling for their bellies to be filled. Jools, who was experiencing some uncharitable and even nasty thoughts about Bunny Goldman and his lovely clothes, called after her rather desperately, 'Well then, can I call you on the visiphone? I've got your Central Reservation Number.'

'Have you indeed,' she replied. 'Please excuse me, but I have to feed the whooping primates of Cedonia.'

Nuts, nuts and more nuts to the whooping primates of Cedonia, thought Jools as he travelled home across the aerial bridges of the city …

Jools Anton P'ntarr lived with his father, mother and ten-year-old brother Milton in one of the fashionable Troglodyte Dwellings on the northern fringe of the city of Ule … Jools' mother had warned all her children never, *never* to refer to their home as a cave, especially not in company. His mother was a dedicated snob.

His folks happened to be away from home at the present time, enjoying a holiday break on Ithica Three. The brochure had promised 'Stunning volcanic sunsets by the light of *two* moons', but Jools had opted to stay at home, get up late, miss lectures, and write poetry of all things about Whatsername.

He summoned Uncle Jerome on the visiphone, knowing that it was a matter of pure luck whether he would get an answer, for Uncle Jerome was not like other people. He sometimes sat up all night observing the nocturnal habits of plants. Jools knew that for some reason his mother didn't like Uncle Jerome very much, and even Father referred to his own brother as 'a flawed genius'. Jools suspected that there was maybe a bit of family history that he hadn't got to the bottom of yet, but it didn't bother him. He liked Uncle Jerome.

When his uncle's face appeared on the screen the sharp eyes softened somewhat when they lit on Jools.

'Ah! Good, I thought you might have been one of *them* complaining again. They don't appreciate the beauty of naturally decomposing compost, my boy. You should hear how they say the word "smell".'

War must have broken out with the neighbours again, Jools surmised, 'It's only me, Uncle Jerome.'

'Never say only me, boy. Always think of yourself as the most important cog in the universal scheme of things.'

'I'll try to do that, Uncle Jerome.'

'If there was no you, the world would not exist. Reality is relative.'

'... Uncle Jerome, I wonder could you help me get someone on the visiphone? I've got this person's Central Registration Number but not the Personal Identity Code. I can't make the call without a PIC.'

Up rose the highly mobile eyebrows. 'And you want me to raid the data banks and get it for you, is that the plan?'

'Well ...' said Jools, treading carefully, 'it's just that I've heard Mother say you know how to do these things. She says you've got an illegal hoard of ... you know ... special equipment. She says you didn't hand back a lot of technology when they gave you the sack that time.'

'Never mind what your mother says. I wonder why you're so desperate for me to invade someone's privacy like this? What's her CRN?'

'HM 86 38 94 B,' said Jools with a blush – he'd been most careful to keep gender out of the conversation.

'Well, we'll see. Goodbye.'

The revolting wheebler escaped from her pen during the night and got among the general public. There were horrendous scenes. People were trampled underfoot and others fainted clean away as Dot turned herself into a worm two kilometres long and surrounded the Ecology building. But help was at hand. To the astonishment of all who were privileged to be there that day, Jools Anton P'ntarr donned rubber gloves and rolled it up like a hose-pipe and returned the wheebler to the trustees of the Inner-Space Menagerie. They were so delighted that they made him an honorary member of staff and he was able to see Whatsername every day.

He woke up in a sweat, quivering with fear at the thought of what he'd just done. He might have had 1,000 volts up his arm and been fried to a frazzle.

A flickering screen caught his eye. It said:

*Try AZD after CRN. Good Luck.*

Good old Uncle Jerome!

From *Jealous Jools and Dominique* by Sam McBratney

1.  Spend about **12 minutes** on this question. Use evidence from lines 1–26 to answer the following question.

    How has the writer used the setting as the story begins?

    [8 marks]

2.  Spend about **15 minutes** on this question. Use evidence from the whole passage to answer this question.

    What sort of a boy is Jools Anton P'ntarr?

    [10 marks]

3.  Spend about **18 minutes** on this question. Use evidence from the whole passage to answer this question.

    This is the opening to a book. How has the writer started to develop a story that sustains our interest.

    You should write about:

    *   the way in which the story is told from Jools's point of view
    *   how the events develop
    *   the humour in the story
    *   the use of words and phrases.

    [12 marks]

\* See **Checklists!** on page 88 for a list of possible points.

# Paper 1 Section B: Writing

There will be one question on this section of the paper – it is the fourth and final question on this two-hour paper.

This section carries the same number of marks as Section A so you should allow the same amount of time for it, 60 minutes. Don't fall into the trap of spending too much time on Section A.

# Question 4: Writing to review, analyse and comment

This question will take the form of an essay. The audience is the examiner and the purpose is to demonstrate your ability to **review, analyse and comment** on a given issue. You can present your own strongly held opinions on the topic, but if you do, remember that your essay should also present an awareness of the viewpoints that may be held by others.

Let's look at a typical question 4:

4. Present your views on the following question:

**Is it right to have a National Lottery?**

Below is a range of opinions about the National Lottery. The examiner wants you to review the points that you consider to be important along with any ideas of your own. Analyse these in an extended piece of writing. You will be expected to include your own comments and conclusions on the topic.

- *Lots of 'good causes' get extra money.*
- Some people are tempted to spend more on the Lottery than they can afford.
- *It's only a bit of harmless fun.*
- The National Lottery is only gambling made respectable.

> You are directed to consider the pointers that are given below, but you are also expected to bring your own ideas and impressions into your answer.

> The issue is at the centre of the question. The subject is one that will be accessible to a 16-year-old audience.

> The audience is specified – you are writing for the examiner.

> This stimulus material is normally balanced, as here, where two of the points are supportive of the Lottery and two take a negative stance.

# Using your time most effectively

You have 60 minutes to answer this question. Aim to write *at least* two sides. Remember, trying to write too much can sometimes be as damaging to your cause as writing too little!

## Planning your answer:

- take about 10–15 minutes to look at the issue. As you are thinking about it, jot down your ideas. You could use the next page of your answer booklet. This is your rough work and as you will not be directly credited for it, don't waste time either writing too much (it's only a plan) or worrying about how neat it is! Cross out this page when you've finished your essay

- what is your opinion on the topic?

- consider both sides of the issue

- can you logically group the prompts you've been given and develop them?

- do you have any relevant anecdotes or personal experiences that you can use in your answer?

- organise your ideas so that there will be a logical flow to your discussion.

## Writing your answer:

- follow your plan through, that way the work will be organised and have a logical structure – it will come across as a piece of controlled writing

- try to make your writing lively and interesting to read

- take care with spelling, punctuation, variety in sentence structure and variety in sentence openings

- make a point of linking your paragraphs

- if you have any spare time, re-read your answer; we all make mistakes when we are working under pressure! Don't be scared to make corrections, there are no marks for tidiness – the examiner will be impressed by corrections that improve the quality of your writing!

# 'Dos and don'ts'

- Avoid the typically dull opening:

  'In this essay I am going to look at both sides of the issue of the National Lottery. I will begin by looking at the points in favour of the National Lottery.'

- Another less than impressive tactic is to open a new paragraph by simply copying out the next prompt from the question:

  'Lots of "good causes" get extra money. This is true and I agree with good causes getting the money ...'

- Challenging or engaging the reader through the use of a rhetorical question can be a lively and effective means of developing attention:

  'Do you think state-sponsored gambling is morally correct?'

- Make use of effective connectives and links:

'Whilst many see nothing wrong in playing the National Lottery, there are others who believe that ...' or 'At the same time it has to be recognised that not everyone can afford to play ...'

- Try to conclude strongly:

'Perhaps it is time the government stopped using the National Lottery as a back-door means of propping up essential services!'

# Time to get practical!

Below are some typical exam questions that you can tackle. Allow yourself one hour in which to complete each of the writing assignments. Remember to present both sides of the case – feel free to conclude by presenting your own point of view. See **Checklists!** on page 88 for a list of possible points.

## Practical session 1.4.1

Present your views on the following question:

### Is it a good idea to have prefects in schools?

Below is a range of opinions about school prefects. The examiner wants you to review the points that you consider to be important along with any ideas of your own. Analyse these in an extended piece of writing. You will be expected to include your own comments and conclusions on the topic.

*It's only right that the most trusted and experienced pupils should be given a share in the running of the school.*

Some prefects are worse than the teachers! They often abuse their authority.

*Being a prefect helps to teach final year pupils a sense of responsibility.*

Prefects get very little in the way of reward for all they do.

## Practical session 1.4.2

Present your views on the following controversial comment:

### Young people today are often a disgrace to society!

Below is a range of opinions about modern young people. The examiner wants you to review the points that you consider to be important along with any ideas of your own. Analyse these in an extended piece of writing. You will be expected to include your own comments and conclusions on the topic.

*They're so selfish! They're only interested in going to clubs and discos.*

Older people never had to cope with all the pressures facing today's youngsters.

*Their language on the street is absolutely appalling!*

Young people *are* responsible and caring. They do a lot of good work for charities.

## Practical session 1.4.3

# PRACTICE PAPER

## Paper 1: Section B

This section tests **writing** skills: to **review, analyse and comment**.

- Write in a way that suits the task.

- To answer this question effectively, you should aim to write **at least two sides**.

- Leave enough time to re-read your work so that you can make any changes you feel are necessary.

4. Present your views on the following topic:

   **The present school holiday system needs to be changed, urgently. The two months holiday in the summer is far too long.**

   Below is a range of opinions about school holidays. The examiner wants you to review the points that you consider to be important along with any ideas of your own. Analyse these in an extended piece of writing. You will be expected to include your own comments and conclusions on the topic.

   *The present summer holiday is too long. Kids get bored by the start of August.*

   Most parents have their annual holidays during July or August. The present system allows children and their parents to be on holiday at the same time.

   *Schools could reduce heating bills by having longer holidays at Christmas or Easter, rather than in the summer.*

   Older pupils use the long summer holiday to earn extra money through part-time jobs, and many of these jobs are only available during the summer months.

   [30 marks]

\* See **Checklists!** on page 88 for a list of possible points.

# Paper 2 Section A: Writing

There will be one question on this section of the paper – it is the first question on this two-hour paper. Remember to manage your time properly. This section is worth the same number of marks as Section B; make sure you stick to the time limit of 60 minutes!

# Question 1: Writing to inform, explain and describe

This question may require you to write in one of a variety of forms – an article for your school magazine; a speech to other pupils or parents; a letter to a friend or perhaps a newspaper; or, a personal essay for the examiner. You will be clearly told which form you are to use and who your target audience is to be.

It is extremely important to employ the required form and reflect an appreciation of the specified audience in your use of language and control of tone.

Of course the real audience for the piece of writing will be the examiner but he/she will be assessing how successful you are in writing for the particular audience you have been given. Always keep the audience in mind!

The purpose to **inform, explain and describe** is going to require you to make use of your own experiences as a basis for your writing – don't be afraid to draw upon these!

Let's look at a typical question 1:

> The form of writing required is specified. It is a speech of welcome so the tone of your writing is specified.

> The audience is defined – this is very important. Always keep it in mind as you write.

1. Write a speech welcoming a group of sixteen-year-old American exchange students to your school or college. In it, inform them about arrangements for their week's stay and some of the highlights to which they may look forward.

> You are told to **inform** your young guests about two things: the arrangements and some of the highlights of their visit. This will require considerable personal development.

# Using your time most effectively

Again, as with the writing task in Paper 1, you have 60 minutes for this question. Aim to write *at least two sides*, between two and three would be about average. Remember attempting to write too much can sometimes be as damaging as writing too little!

## Planning your answer:

- take about 10–15 minutes to plan your answer. As you are thinking about the topic, jot down your ideas. You could use the next page of your answer booklet. This is your rough work and as you will not be directly credited for it, don't waste time either writing too much (it's only a plan) or worrying about how neat it is! Cross out this page when you've finished your essay

- keep the purpose of the writing and the audience at the forefront of your thinking

- use your planning time to think about how you can most effectively meet the demands of the topic

- if you are given any prompts, consider how you can develop them

- do you have any relevant anecdotes or personal experiences that you can use?

- organise your ideas so that there will be a logical flow to your writing.

## Writing your answer:

- re-read the comparable section 'Writing your answer' on p. 41 – make use of this advice.

# 'Dos and don'ts'

- Make sure to match the writing form to the purpose:
  - if you're writing a speech, make sure you address your audience immediately – '*It's a real pleasure for me to welcome our friends from America to our school today …*' and as you finish – '*I hope you guys are looking forward to the week as much as we are — thank you.*'
  - a letter to a newspaper has the readers of the paper as its audience – you are not actually writing to the Editor!
  - an article, say for a school magazine, would generally have its own heading. Thinking about your audience will help with tone and choice of words and phrases
  - if you are asked to write about something from your own experience, say, 'The Best Day of My Life', don't decide to make something up! You will have enough to do writing in a fluent and engaging manner without giving yourself the added trouble of having to concoct the subject matter as well!

- Choose words and phrases that are appropriate to the audience: some slang would be acceptable if you've been asked to write to a close friend of your own age but not if the audience is teachers, parents or the general public.

- Structure your writing in paragraphs: remember to use your plan to develop your answer in paragraphs.

- Make use of effective connectives and links to give a sense of organisation to your piece: smooth and logical connections add fluency and will impress the examiner.
- Bring variety to your sentence structure: showing control of sentence length and structure improves the quality of your writing and will help to engage the examiner's interest and should lead to increased marks!

# Time to get practical!

Stick to the one-hour time limit! Below are some typical exam questions that you can tackle. Remember the key to successfully completing this section of the exam lies in:

a   recognising the form you have to use and understanding the different demands of that writing

b   taking note of the audience you have been asked to write for and shaping your work to suit the specified audience.

See **Checklists!** on page 89 for a list of possible points.

## Practical session 2.1.1

1.  Write an essay for the examiner about your favourite book or piece of music.

    In your answer:

    - describe your choice of book or music
    - explain why it is important to you
    - inform the examiner about any other relevant details.

## Practical session 2.1.2

1.  As part of an introduction to their new school, you have been asked to speak to the Year 8 pupils about your time at the school.

    Write the talk you would give. You should aim to help them feel welcome and to encourage a sense of pride in their new school.

    Here are some ideas to help you:

    - highlight the positive aspects of your school
    - outline your own achievements
    - tell about some amusing/important incidents.

## Practical session 2.1.3

1.  Write an article for your school magazine about an interesting event which took place in your school.

    In your article you should:

    - inform the reader about the preparations made for this event
    - explain what happened and who took part
    - describe the atmosphere at the event.

Practical session 2.1.4

# PRACTICE PAPER

## Paper 2: Section A

This section tests **writing** skills: to **inform, explain and describe**.

- Write in a way that suits the task.
- The answer should be developed fully. You will be expected to write **at least two sides** in the answer booklet.
- Leave enough time to **re-read your work** so that you can make any changes you feel are necessary.

---

1. Write a letter to a pen pal from another country about the place where you live. You should aim to write in a lively and informative manner.

   In your letter you should:

   - describe your local area
   - inform the reader about any major attractions
   - explain what's good and bad about living where you do.

   [30 marks]

*See **Checklists!** on page 89 for a list of possible points.

# Paper 2 Section B: Reading

There are three questions to be answered in this section of the paper: numbers 2–4.

# Question 2: The use of presentational devices

The first of these questions will carry 8, 9 or 10 marks. It is not the most demanding question in this part of the paper and therefore it is one from which you should aim to score heavily.

Let's look at a typical question 2:

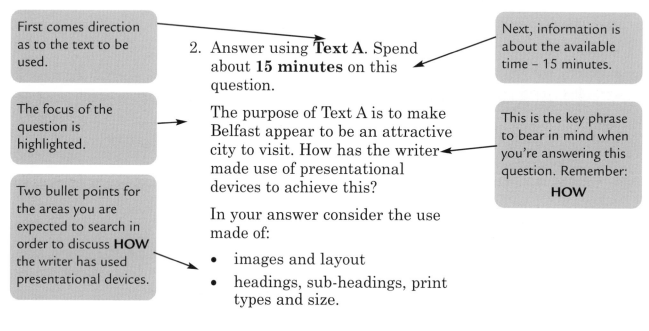

First comes direction as to the text to be used.

The focus of the question is highlighted.

Two bullet points for the areas you are expected to search in order to discuss **HOW** the writer has used presentational devices.

2. Answer using **Text A**. Spend about **15 minutes** on this question.

The purpose of Text A is to make Belfast appear to be an attractive city to visit. How has the writer made use of presentational devices to achieve this?

In your answer consider the use made of:

- images and layout
- headings, sub-headings, print types and size.

Next, information is about the available time – 15 minutes.

This is the key phrase to bear in mind when you're answering this question. Remember: **HOW**

## Using your time most effectively

The following approach is intended to enable you to answer effectively. It is designed for the question above. Probably the easiest, quickest and therefore most effective way of sorting out what you are going to write is to annotate your text as you quickly analyse it – whatever helps you to organise your answer quickly and efficiently!

a   Take some time to analyse the areas of the text referred to in the bullet points.

- How do the images and the layout impact on you?

    *What first catches your eye? What effect does the main image have? Are there other images – what is their function? What use is made of colour? Does the layout support the images? Are there bullet points? Is it organised in text boxes or short or long paragraphs? Does it help to make the text 'user-friendly'?*

- What effect do the headings, sub-headings, print types and size have?

   *Do they help to support the central message? Do they act as a contrast? Is use made of alliteration? Do they support the tone of the writing? Is use made of an amusing pun? Does the font, the font style or the print size catch the attention – is there a mix of these?*

b  Use the remainder of your time to concisely write your answer. Remember the focus of the question – HOW these presentational devices have been used!

# Final advice

- You have got to be confident enough to look at what the writer has done with presentation and layout and briefly present your analysis of it. You will be awarded very few marks for simply saying that there is a picture, for example – what purpose do you think it serves and what effect does the writer hope to gain by including it? Keep the focus on the presentational devices and their intended purpose.

- If you are presented with bullet points, use them as guidance for your answer and stick to the time limits.

# Time to get practical!

The following texts and questions offer you the opportunity to practise analysing presentational devices. The leaflets and article are in black and white but you can find colour versions of them at www.hoddernorthernireland.co.uk/english.htm

## Practical session 2.2.1

Take 7–8 minutes to carefully analyse the leaflet on pp. 50–51.

An annotated sample answer has been included on p. 56 – it is intended to help you see the 'dos and don'ts' of answering this type of question.

You can either write your own answer to the question before reading the annotated answer or simply read the response and the commentary – whichever you think will be most useful for you.

**Remember**, you can find colour versions of the leaflets at www.hoddernorthernireland.co.uk/english.htm

The front cover

The back of the leaflet

The inner flap

## Text A

Above is the outer cover of a three-sectioned A4 leaflet. This is followed on the opposite page by the inner spread of the leaflet.

The inside spread

Answer using **Text A**. Spend about **15 minutes** on this question.

The purpose of Text A is to make The Dunluce Centre appear to be an exciting attraction to visit.

How has the writer made use of presentational devices to achieve this?

In your answer consider the use made of:

- images, layout and use of colour
- headings, sub-headings, print types and size.

See the sample answer on page 56.

# Practical session 2.2.2

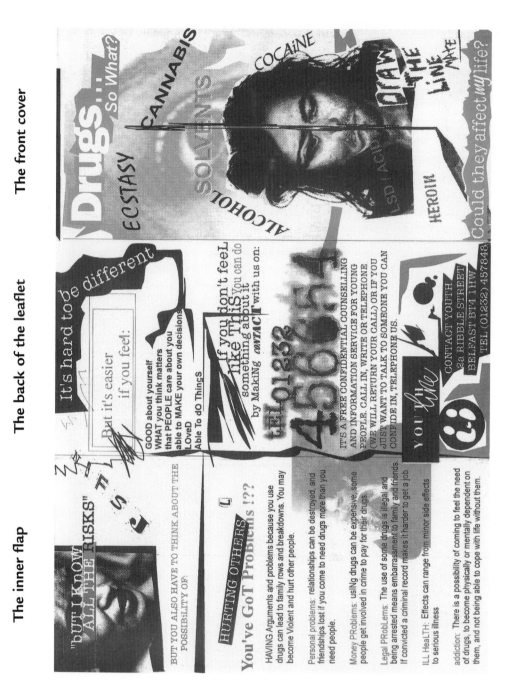

Study the leaflet on these pages, for 7–8 minutes, before answering the question that follows.

**Remember**, you can find colour versions of the leaflets at www.hoddernorthernireland.co.uk/english.htm

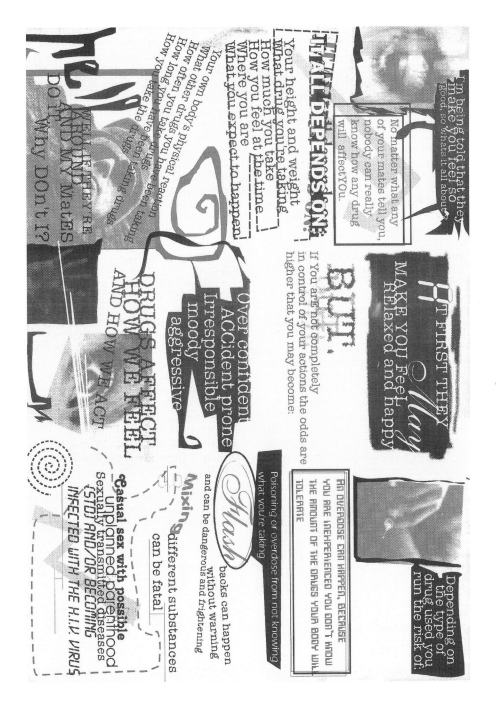

The inside spread

Spend about **15 minutes** on this question.

The purpose of this text is to confront the issue of drug taking. How has the writer made use of presentational devices to achieve this?

In your answer consider the use made of:

- images, layout and use of colour
- print types and size, headings and sub-headings.

See **Checklists!** on page 89 for a list of possible points.

## Practical session 2.2.3

### CORFU

**We were on a long car journey the first time my son, Joe, heard a story tape of Gerald Durrell's *My Family and Other Animals*.** He was thrilled… I kept glancing back at him; he looked amazed. How could this writer know how he felt when he watched a spider, or dreamt of bringing home a wounded bird? …

Joe was six. Two years later … we set off for Corfu … Durrell once said, famously, that if he could give any child a gift, it would be his own Corfu childhood. We were hoping to taste a tiny sliver of it.

We stayed at The White House, an old fisherman's house where Gerald's brother Lawrence and his young wife Nancy lived … Now converted into a restaurant and an airy upstairs apartment, it sits 'like a dice', as Lawrence Durrell put it, on one edge of the bay of Kalami on the developed but still lovely northeast coast of the island.

Just as Gerald himself sometimes elaborated the truth, or muddled his chronology for the sake of a better yarn, so does the very active Durrell Tourist Board, conveniently merging Gerald's life on the island with that of Lawrence … So, on our first morning in The White House, indeed every morning of the holiday, we were greeted with ship's hootings and music, then bellowed announcements through a loudspeaker that, ''Ere to your left, ees the famous White House, in the lovely, peaceful bay of Kalami, home of the very famous writer Gerald Durrell.' Then the pirate ships, stuffed with roasting young holidaymakers, would lurch off to a cacophony of techno beats.

The White House … is where Lawrence Durrell wrote *Prospero's Cell*. Lawrence did big ideas and grand themes. He did Art. He didn't do tortoises. And tortoises were what we were after.

By now Joe's wish list was growing: he'd decided what he really, really wanted to see was a freshwater turtle – a terrapin. He also wanted to find a snake, a Scops owl, and countless sorts of lizards, newts, spiders and grasshoppers. His sisters – Flora, his twin, and Molly, 3 – tolerated his passions, but drew the line at snakes. For the first few days, Joe was a boy possessed. Every waking moment was spent searching undergrowth and walls, perpetually hopeful, his hopes inevitably dashed. Sebastian, my husband, was becoming worryingly obsessed, too …

We hired a boat … It was our salvation. It took everyone's minds off tortoises. We could phutt-phutt-phutt our way around the coast, dropping anchor where we liked, diving with great multicoloured schools of fish and playing at being as jet-set as the owners of the appropriately named *Awesome* – one of many yachts for the super-rich we gawped at as they idled around the edges of Corfu. Joe and Flora, at 8, could do some proper snorkelling and would splutter to the surface amazed. Molly would dive down with her goggles and waterwings, like a Day-Glo underwater cherub.

Everywhere we went in our little boat, we met children, and children and more children. We would moor at a tavern for lunch, Molly often asleep in her life-jacket in the bottom of the boat, and would order our food while the children made instant friends. They have never had such a happily sociable holiday …

So Corfu was going well – in all but one respect. We'd tried to placate Joe with some disastrously unsuccessful line fishing, but we were running out of time. In Kalami village, we bought a little guide to the Durrells' Corfu, and it turned out to be a delight. My husband was taken with the idea of the Chessboard Fields. A favourite haunt of the young Gerald, Durrell described them as a watery wonderland, a lush patchwork of allotments criss-crossed by an elaborate series of ditches and waterways, plopping with the sound of plump green frogs and freshwater turtles. This surely was Joe Country.

We followed the instructions in the book: the fields were on the edge of a lagoon, right by the airport. We parked the car near a petrol station on a scrubby road. Things couldn't have looked less promising. It was 6 o'clock in the evening, with that intense but mellow sunlight that comes at the end of a hot day. As we walked, we entered a different Corfu: no pirate ships, no boat hire, no sea-view apartments. So close to the din of the runway, the Chessboard Fields were unexploitable for tourism – here was Gerald's Corfu, preserved. We passed a tiny, ancient, walnut-faced lady, with a donkey laden with vegetables from her allotment. Then an old man, watering his plot at the end of the day. They nodded, but looked surprised to see our little troupe. The greenery became more abundant, almost tropical. Vines hung low with black grapes. We followed the waterways, eyes scouring the water's surface for action. The occasional plop, scudding waterboatmen, a buzz in the air.

Then Joe saw something in the water. He was sure, quite sure, it was a terrapin. Nobody believed him, but he has a naturalist's eyes and powers of concentration. Sebastian straddled the muddy

# ALL CREATURES

A trip to Corfu was bound to be a Durrell-inspired affair for a boy who loves nature.

banks and lowered his hands in the water, with Joe leaning over, their two heads together. Then, with much sploshing and excitement, out he came, a wonderful, big, yellowy-green terrapin, held in turn with much reverence by each of the children until he was returned to the cool, muddy sanctuary of the water.

In a holiday full of great moments, of cool dives and salty swims, of boats and walks and beachside meals, this was the best moment of all. The terrapin was wonderful, ancient looking, and dignified. We found him, ourselves, in this golden, special, secret place. Under the deafening roar of jumbos … we had discovered our own unlikely paradise. I will not forget the look of rapture on Joe's face as he held the animal. 'Do you know what I'm doing, Mum,' he said, plucking at the skin on his arm. 'I'm pinching myself, in case it's not real.'

Clockwise from top right: Gerald Durrell (aged 9) with his dog, Roger, soon after his arrival in Corfu in 1935; the little boat moored; Joe with grasshopper; the terrapin; Flora and Joe on board the boat, north of Kalami.

# GREAT AND SMALL

Gill Morgan recounts her family's quest for a turtle.

*The Times Magazine,* 10th January 2004

The material you will be asked to analyse will not always be an advertising brochure. Study this piece from the colour supplement of a newspaper and answer the question below. **Remember,** you can find colour versions of the photos at www.hoddernorthernireland.co.uk/english.htm

This is an article from newspaper magazine. Spend **15 minutes** on this question.

Consider the way in which colour, pictures and layout have been used to develop the reader's interest in this article. See **Checklists!** on page 89 for a list of possible points.

# Sample answer (question 2 on p.51)

An analytical comment on the contrasting use of colour in the leaflet demonstrates an understanding of its effect.

The different illustrations are discussed and their appeal analysed. The potential appeal of these in relation to the intended audience is assessed.

This paragraph comments on layout, headings and use of fonts. The final sentence relates the remarks back to the focus of the question.

Recognises the link that is used between colour and the images in the leaflet.

Notice that there is analysis of each of the images – not simply description.

The final observation is another analytical comment, this time on the effect of a sub-heading. Notice the way in which it is tied into HOW the leaflet attempts to create its desired effect.

*The front cover of the leaflet with its plain white background, three headings and logos are, in terms of presentation, understated in comparison to the rest of the leaflet. However, inside bright colours immediately catch the eye and this provides the leaflet with an instant source of interest and appeal for any potential reader.*

*These vibrant colours lead the reader into the major presentational feature, the illustrations. The central 'Finn McCool' image, interestingly, is not a photograph but rather an artist's impression — presumably to make the attraction appear more dramatic and hence appealing. The 'Turbo Tours' illustration features cartoon-like characters leaping out from a cinema screen in front of children who are enjoying the hair-raising experience. This would certainly appeal to youngsters who enjoy such 'white-knuckle' experiences. A drawing of a pirate, with clichéd knife in mouth, is likely to attract children to the 'Treasure Fortress'.*

*The layout of each of the three sections of the pamphlet has an attractive purple stripe featuring headings that run vertically. These use a large, quirky, mediaeval-looking font that ties in well with the 'Finn McCool' and 'Treasure Fortress' attractions. These not only help to guide the reader through the pamphlet, but further develop the sense of interest and excitement that the leaflet is attempting to generate.*

*The unusual placing of the sub-heading with its dramatic message 'Live ... Adventure'; its brilliant yellow background and variety of font sizes is another appealing ingredient that aims to further excite the reader.*

## A summary of the answer:

There is a range of perceptive and supported points presented. The answer, as well as being characterised by perceptive analysis, maintains a clear focus on the question and consequently is relevant throughout. The areas mentioned in the bullet points are clearly reflected in the response.

# Question 3: Analysing non-fiction

Question 3 will ask you to read and respond to a non-fiction text. Texts you are most likely to meet are: letters, diary entries, travel writing, biographies and autobiographies.

Many media texts, such as advertisements and newspaper articles, set out to inform and/or persuade their target-audiences. Non-fiction writing can also be informative and persuasive but it engages the reader in other ways as well. This is frequently achieved by:

- the reader becoming absorbed in the uniquely personal quality of the writing which often reflects the personality of the writer
- entertaining the reader by using humour and/or a lively style of writing
- capturing the reader's interest through careful structuring of sentences and paragraphs to develop thoughts, ideas, opinions and arguments.

The activities in this section are designed to take you through the distinctive features of non-fiction writing, examining how these can:

- create interest and enjoyment
- appeal to the reader's senses and emotions
- influence the reader's views and opinions.

First, let's look at a typical question 3:

Timing is of the utmost importance. Note the recommended time and adhere to this.

This question will deal with **one** of the two texts in this section of the **paper**. This tells you which text you MUST base your answer on.

3. Spend **15 minutes** on this question. Use the piece of travel writing to answer the question.

The writer has used an entertaining style to interest the reader. How has he achieved this?

In your answer, comment on:

- the personal nature of the writing
- the use of humour
- the variety in sentence structure and use of paragraphing.

This statement is the central focus of the question and should not be ignored. It tells you what the writer has accomplished.

Use these bullet points to structure your answer. They are telling you what the examiner wants you to write about.

Your task is to analyse **HOW** the writer has succeeded in writing an entertaining and interesting piece.

Select examples of these features from the text and then comment on **HOW** they have contributed in achieving what the writer intended. Always support your points in this manner to show your understanding of the writer's skills.

# Using your time most effectively

a   Use some of your 15-minute time allocation to analyse the areas of the text referred to in the bullet points. You will see how significant these bullets are in directing you in practical sessions 2.3.1. and 2.3.2 below. You are allowed to annotate your copy of the non-fiction text in order to help your planning process.

b   Use the remainder of your time to concisely write your answer. Remember to keep the focus on the question.

# Time to get practical!

As this is one of the 'new' questions, the **practical session 2.3.1** is followed by a thorough analysis – its purpose is to let you see how you might build up an appropriate answer.

## Practical session 2.3.1

**Spend 15 minutes on this question. This is an engaging piece of writing. How has the writer made it interesting for the reader?**

**In your answer comment on the following:**

- **the personal nature of the writing**
- **the lively style employed by the writer**
- **the variety in sentence structure and use of paragraphing.**

In this piece of travel writing, the writer describes what happened on her recent adventure holiday ...

Hold on tight: here comes the most memorable experience of your life. It's going to suck your breath away and crunch your nerves. There may even be a moment when you'll be wishing you were anywhere else on earth. But then you'll feel the adrenaline rush. And afterwards: what a story!

Our thirst for new holiday thrills seems unrelenting. If something is high, we want to jump off it; if it's fast, we want to ride on it; if it's just plain dangerous – yep sign us up. Apparently, you can swim with man-eating sharks in the South Atlantic, spend a month without water in the Utah desert, or tackle perilous river rapids in New Zealand – without the aid of a boring old boat!

But why, in an act of madness, did I decide to throw myself down a bobsleigh run at 60mph while balanced on a child-sized sled? I volunteered because my typical week consists of shifting from office chair to sofa, with an occasional detour to a bar stool in-between. Time, I thought, for something more daring. Want to know what happened? Here we go then!

Dazzling sunlight blazes in the cloudless Norwegian sky. I am in Lillehammer Olympic Park, preparing to launch myself – headfirst – down the tunnel of ice that is its bobsleigh run. There is no safety belt. There are no brakes. I'd give anything to be back in the office right now.

My instructor is Tony Wallington, former Olympic bobsleigh competitor. Tony has been preparing me for the ordeal ahead by showing me footage of professional lunatics hurtling along at 90mph. There is also a safety presentation, but, unfortunately, I don't listen to any of it.

This is not because I feel over-confident, nor because of any fault of Tony's whose experience and knowledge are inspiring. I do not listen because fear is causing me to block everything else out.

Tony walks me out along the terrifyingly steep 1,710-metre skeleton track. It's a coiling structure of metal and concrete, largely covered to protect its coating of ice from the fierce sunlight. He gestures towards a towering convex wall.

'This is bend 13, where the force reaches 5G,' he says. Observing my ashen face, he smiles reassuringly: 'So long as you do as I've told you, you'll be fine.' I don't tell him I've heard nothing he's said.

Ten minutes later, I am clad in overalls and crash helmet and lying face down at the mouth of the tunnel, neck straining to lift my face above the icy floor. Tony is gripping my ankles, offering final words of advice.

'Never stick your arm out – you'll break it. Remember to steer yourself by looking where you want to go.'

I stare at a stretch of ice, seemingly cut short by a solid wall.

'Ready?'

Definitely not ready. Yet, strangely, I hear my mouth issue a pathetic 'Yes'.

A quick shove and I lurch forward, my shoulder slamming against the ice. I whip around a corner and hit a 180-degree bend full on, shooting up the wall. I can't scream because centrifugal forces are pushing down on my head, clamping my jaw shut.

The track drops into a straight. I'm out of control, pinballing into the unknown, and suddenly I understand why I am not thrown from the sled beneath me. I am welded to it by a crushing force, which causes nausea to flare a warning from my compressed stomach. Juddering deeper into the tunnel, the rumbling sound of the sled becomes a thunderous clatter. It feels like being strapped under a runaway train.

At the famous bend 13, the pressure becomes so great that I can no longer support my head. Momentarily, my chin scrapes the ice. I'm supposed to be 'looking where I want to go', but I'm petrified. Tears streak my face at horizontal angles. I can't seem to wrench my gaze from the fast-approaching wall.

This is it ... the end! I swerve, tossed into the air then hammering back down to earth. Then, suddenly, it really is the end. I am spat out into the sunshine and trundle to a halt.

I am in shock. I can do no more than roll onto my back, lungs fighting to compensate for the fact that I have not drawn breath in over a minute, and try to make sense of the confused mess of images and noise in my mind.

Hands appear from above, hauling my battered body over the edge. I stand up. Tony rushes over to hug me and I start to laugh. Heart thumping, limbs throbbing, ears rattling, one word sings in my head: again, again, again.

From *The Sunday Times*, 7th March 2004, by Miranda Whittam

The following checklists are built around the bullet points – just as your answer should be! They are *extremely* detailed to give you as much guidance as possible. Having planned your answer, you will only have about 10 minutes in which to write it.

## The personal nature of the writing:

☞ the fact that the writer is giving an account of a highly dramatic event she was personally involved in captures the reader's interest

☞ the use of present tense gives the reader the impression of living the experience along with the narrator as it is happening. This has the effect of involving the reader directly in all the excitement as he/she is taken along for the ride too. The sense of immediacy this creates gives this writing real impact

☞ note the use of first person narrative from the third paragraph on. This allows the writer to develop her thoughts and feelings as well as to describe what she could see and hear. The reader is caught up in the events from the narrator's perspective and this, in turn, helps to convey a sense of the danger/exhilaration the writer experienced

☞ the personal nature of the piece allows the reader to empathise with the writer which further involves the reader in her adventure. For example, she freely confesses how afraid she was and this is something with which the reader can easily identify

☞ the internal monologue as she is hurtling along the ice tunnel is extremely effective in sustaining the reader's interest. Revealing her innermost thoughts and feelings helps to develop a bond between the writer and the reader. Because the reader has been taken into the writer's confidence in this way, he/she takes more interest and feels more involved in the narrative

☞ she uses some personal details to reinforce the sense of drama/create more impact such as the nausea she feels and how she can't hold up her head.

## The lively style employed:

☞ the informal approach taken in the opening paragraph sets the cheerful/enthusiastic tone which is characteristic of the piece

☞ the writer speaks directly to the reader in the opening paragraphs in a very friendly/informal way: 'Hold on tight'/'Here we go then!' This helps the reader feel he/she is being invited to participate in the thrill of the ride

☞ she adds to her narrative with humorous touches such as the examples of adventure holidays, her description of her 'typical week' and reference to 'a boring old boat'

☞ the use of hyperbole/exaggeration for humorous effect helps to make the piece engaging to read. For example, references such as the 'child-sized sled', 'professional lunatics' and 'an act of madness'

☞ the simile 'like being strapped … runaway train' conveys a sense of danger and drama

☞ the humorous observation of the swings in the writer's emotions from fear and shock through to elation and pleasure at her achievement also helps to sustain interest

☞ the writer pokes gentle fun at herself: 'I hear my mouth issue a pathetic "Yes".' As well as adding to the reader's enjoyment, this also evokes the reader's sympathy for the writer's predicament

☞ it is worth mentioning how exclamation marks are used to help enliven the writing as well as heightening the sense of tension and drama at particular moments.

## The variety in sentence structure and use of paragraphing:

☞ the opening two paragraphs encourage the reader to think about the thrills of an adventure holiday

☞ the third paragraph is a linking one which the writer uses to introduce her own adventurous exploit to the reader

☞ the rhetorical question at the beginning of this paragraph is used to draw the reader into her decision. The paragraph ends with a direct appeal to the reader to share the experience alongside the writer

☞ the sequence of events as they unfold to a dramatic climax absorb the reader throughout the whole episode

☞ direct speech is used to sensationalise the writer's bobsleigh run. Her thoughts are contrasted with the words of her instructor to enhance the sense of daring and drama

☞ short factual sentences also help dramatise the experience: 'There is no safety belt. There are no brakes'

☞ a mixture of long and short sentences, along with a series of short paragraphs adds variety to the piece as well as making it undemanding to read

☞ towards the end, the short sentence 'I am in shock' is followed by a very long sentence. At this point the writer is gasping/gulping for breath. The length and rhythm of this sentence is clearly meant to reflect a sense of her breathlessness

☞ the conclusion effectively conveys the writer's high spirits and delight

☞ the repetition at the end of the final sentence successfully keeps the reader involved right to the end as it helps communicate the writer's enthusiasm and exhilaration and this is hard to ignore. It also suggests a sense of her heart thumping with exertion.

# Practical session 2.3.2

This text is followed by an annotated answer that will be useful guidance regarding the level of analysis required in your response. You may wish to attempt to answer the question first before reading the sample answer.

**Spend about 15 minutes on this question. How has the writer captured the reader's interest?**

**You should consider:**

- **the personal nature of the account**
- **the light-hearted tone**
- **the variety in sentence structure and use of paragraphing.**

This is what a mother wrote in her diary about one of the challenges of parenthood …

I have resisted allowing her to have her ears pierced, or to get a television set for her bedroom – so how did I come to allow my 11-year-old daughter to have her own mobile phone?

Before you screech 'bad mother', don't worry – I've already stamped that across my forehead. In my defence, all I can say is that I gave in to the most intense pressure yet. Perhaps anyone who has battled with a persuasive 11-year-old hell bent on getting her own way might have just a *little* sympathy.

Two years ago, it was the Disney store she hung around; that gave way to The Link and Vodafone. What amazed me was how much knowledge she had about mobile phones. If she studied her Maths and History as eagerly, she would be at Oxford University by now!

The health issue was a major worry. I didn't want my precious child's developing brain being microwaved. But she reassured me that a doctor's daughter at school had been allowed one, and that her sister was getting one too.

As I drive home late at night, I eventually decided to get a phone to keep in the car. 'Wow, a Nokia,' she said. 'These are brilliant. You can play games on this one …' She was off with it before I'd even worked out how to switch it on. I watched open-mouthed as she programmed its ringing tone, all the phone numbers I might need in an emergency, sent a text message to a friend and settled down to play 'Snake'.

'Get off, it's mine,' I protested weakly. This proved a debatable point during the summer holidays. I began getting text messages asking me if I 'fancied Alex or Ben', and by September, my phone bill had doubled.

I finally came unstuck at half-term. I had promised we could go away, then found we couldn't. After several days of 'Well, pleeeeeease can I get a phone then' and 'Mummy I *must* have a mobile – *everybody* else has one', I cracked. 'Only if you buy it yourself,' I said, exhausted.

With a whoop of joy she grabbed the money she had been saving for a poodle, and we rushed off to the nearest branch of The Link. The assistant didn't seemed fazed at being questioned intensely and knowledgeably about the properties of a Philips as opposed to an Ericsson by a small, pig-tailed girl who hardly reached his chest; it seemed he was used to it.

Eventually, she chose a phone – one which vibrates, is voice-activated and which tells fortunes! She was beside herself with glee.

Now, I suppose, I can see some advantages. The phone does keep her quiet and it is teaching her about budgeting. She has to save up for her Pay and Go top ups, so can't use it without some thought (I actually felt sorry for her when she announced that she had 28 messages, but couldn't afford to retrieve them).

I was also heartened by recent reports that said that young girls who have mobiles are spending their pocket money on them rather than sweets, and teenage girls are going without cigarettes for the same reason.

And, at the weekend, I was waiting outside the leisure centre for her and her friend when a bossy traffic warden demanded I buy a pay-and-display ticket. I moved out of sight, phoned my daughter and begged her to hurry up, which she did – thus saving me 60p. Perhaps phones for children aren't such a bad idea.

From the *Daily Telegraph*, by Greer Harris

# Sample answer

Shows appreciation of how the first person narrative engages the reader.

A series of valid comments on the personal nature of the piece of writing.

Some appropriate analysis that is quite well supported and keeps the question in focus.

In these two paragraphs appropriate examples have been selected without really explaining *why* they are funny and *how* they help to add interest.

A sound understanding of how the structure has contributed to the reader's involvement and enjoyment.

More apt comment that could have been linked back to the question.

> *This is a personal situation between a mother and daughter written from the mother's point-of-view. The account of her experiences as a parent takes the form of a private diary and the details she reveals makes the text engaging to read.*
>
> *The use of first person narrative helps the reader become involved as we can all identify with this situation. The writer engages us from the start by listing all the normal things she has resisted allowing her daughter like pierced ears and a television in her bedroom.*
>
> *A lively, informal style is used throughout. This is achieved partly by the light-hearted tone using the writer's thoughts, like, 'Before you screech "bad mother"'. The writer appears to be talking to the reader and this style keeps us interested.*
>
> *The writer over-exaggerates at times. She refers to how her daughter would be at Oxford University and how she worried that her child's brain might get 'microwaved'.*
>
> *The writer tells the reader about how she received text messages from her daughter's friends asking if she 'fancied Alex or Ben'. Equally the idea of a 'small pig-tailed girl' discussing phones with an adult shop assistant in The Link is funny.*
>
> *How the text is structured also helps to make it interesting. The opening paragraph reveals that she has already given in to her daughter's demands. The final three paragraphs show how the writer has come to see the advantages of mobile phones. The piece finishes off with the comment 'Perhaps phones for children aren't such a bad idea'. In between, the text is broken up into small paragraphs, each telling the reader a little more about how the girl eventually gets her own way and even succeeds in changing her mother's mind.*
>
> *There is variety in the way sentences are structured. For example, there is direct speech, some words are in italics and part of a sentence is in brackets. She sometimes uses exclamation marks to add emphasis and this is effectively combined with the rule of three: '... one which vibrates, is voice activated and which tells fortunes!'*

## A summary of the answer:

This is a competent response. The bullet points were well employed to structure an answer that identified and then considered a range of features of the writer's style. The tendency to refer to appropriate examples but not to analyse how these contributed to an engaging piece of writing is where the response could have been improved.

The following sessions offer you a series of examples to work through. These texts and questions offer you the opportunity to engage with a variety of non-fiction material that will be typical of what you will encounter in your examination. In each case read through the text twice and then allow yourself no more than 15 minutes to plan and write your response. Assess your answer by comparing what you wrote against the appropriate checklist at the back of the book. Learn from this and move on to the next example when you're ready.

## Practical session 2.3.3

**Spend 15 minutes on this question. How has the writer succeeded in engaging the reader?**

**In your response comment on:**

- **the personal nature of the writing**
- **the variety in sentence structure and use of paragraphing.**

In this excerpt the writer is looking back on the type of lessons he enjoyed as a boy when he first arrived in Corfu. George is his teacher.

... George wisely instituted the novel system of outdoor lessons. Some mornings he arrived, carrying a large furry towel, and together we would make our way down through the olive-groves and along the road that was like a carpet of white velvet under its layer of dust. Then we branched off on to a goat-track that ran along the top of miniature cliffs, until it led us to a bay, secluded and small, with a crescent-shaped fringe of white sand running round it. A grove of stunted olives grew there, providing a pleasant shade. From the top of the little cliff the water in the bay looked so still and transparent that it was hard to believe there was any at all. Fishes seemed to drift over the wave-wrinkled sand as though suspended in mid-air; while through six feet of clear water you could see rocks on which anemones lifted frail, coloured arms, and hermit crabs moved, dragging their top-shaped homes.

We would strip beneath the olives and walk out into the warm, bright water, to drift, face down, over the rocks and clumps of seaweed, occasionally diving to bring up something that caught our eye: a shell more brightly coloured than the rest; or a hermit crab of massive proportions, wearing an anemone on his shell, like a bonnet with a pink flower on it ... Treading water and peering down, we could see below the shining, narrow fronds of green and black weeds growing close and tangled, over which we hung like hawks suspended in air above a strange woodland. In the clearing among the weed-bed lay the sea-slugs, perhaps the ugliest of the sea fauna. Some six inches long, they looked exactly like overgrown sausages made out of thick, brown, carunculated [*ribbed*] leather; dim, primitive beasts that just lie in one spot, rolling gently with the sea's swing, sucking in sea water at one end of their bodies and passing it out at the other. The minute vegetable and animal life in the water is filtered off somewhere inside the sausage, and passed to the simple mechanism of the sea-slug's stomach. No one could say that the sea-slugs led interesting lives. Dully they lolled on the sand, sucking in the sea with monotonous regularity. It was hard to believe that these obese creatures could defend themselves in any way, or that they would ever need to, but in fact they had an unusual method of showing their displeasure. Pick them up out of the water, and they would squirt a jet of sea-water out of either end of their bodies, apparently without any muscular effort. It was this water-pistol habit of theirs that led us to invent a game. Each armed with a sea-slug we would make our weapons squirt, noting how and where the water struck the sea. Then we moved over to that spot, and the one who discovered the greatest amount of sea fauna in his area won a point. Occasionally, as in any game, feelings would run high, indignant accusations of cheating would be made and denied. It was then that we found our sea-slugs useful for turning on our opponent. Whenever we had made use of the sea-slugs' services, we always swam out and returned them to their forest of weed. Next time we came down they would still be there, probably in exactly the same position as we had left them, rolling quietly to and fro.

Having exhausted the possibilities of the slugs, we would hunt for new shells for my collection, or hold long discussions on the other fauna we had found; George would suddenly realise that all this, though most enjoyable, could hardly be described as education in the strictest sense of the word, so we would drift back to the shallows and lie there. The lesson then proceeded, while the shoals of little fish would gather about us and nibble gently at our legs ...

The sea was like a warm, silky coverlet that moved my body gently to and fro. There were no waves, only this gentle underwater movement, the pulse of the sea, rocking me softly. Around my legs the coloured fish flicked and trembled, and stood on their heads while they mumbled at me with toothless gums. In the drooping clusters of olives a cicada whispered gently to itself ...

Across the mouth of the bay a sun-bleached boat would pass, rowed by a brown fisherman in tattered trousers, standing in the stern and twisting an oar in the water like a fish's tail. He would raise one hand in lazy salute, and across the still, blue water you could hear the plaintive squeak of the oar ...

From *My Family and Other Animals* by Gerald Durrell

See **Checklists!** on page 89 for a list of possible points.

## Practical session 2.3.4

**Spend 15 minutes on this question. The extract from Steve Fossett's biography is engaging to read. How has this been achieved?**

**Consider the following:**

- **the positive picture created of Steve Fossett's life**
- **the sentence structure and use of paragraphing.**

The following text describes details about the life of the adventurer, Steve Fossett.

As his contemporaries contemplate shuffling along to collect their free bus-passes, Steve Fossett was contemplating a more remarkable journey: sailing around the world in a record 58 days. In 2002, Fossett had already become the first man to circle the world solo in a hot-air balloon and before then had broken 21 other world records. His friend Sir Richard Branson calls him 'the greatest adventurer alive'. But if Peggy, his wife of 35 years, hopes he might now spend a little more time in his slippers, she will be disappointed.

What is it that drives a man to risk a secure retirement? Why can't he get his kicks from golf or bowls, rather than swimming the Channel or climbing Mount Kilimanjaro? Few of us would fancy falling out of the sky minus a parachute (just a so-so day at the office for Fossett).

His passion began at the age of 11 in the Scouts when he climbed a mountain. That spirit never left him: 'I have climbed more than 300 peaks and never get tired of the thrill of standing on top.' But he was into his forties before his mountaineering passion developed into an addiction for what he terms, modestly, 'more adventurous sports' such as car racing at Le Mans and husky racing in Alaska.

He was always a very private man but all that changed when he became the first man to make it solo round the world in a hot-air balloon. Earlier attempts had nearly ended in fatal disaster. 'Ballooning was admittedly very dangerous. The most scary was when my balloon ruptured at 29,000ft off Australia in 1998 and I went down in the Coral Sea. That was barely survivable. I wouldn't expect to survive that twice.'

A parachute would have been useless: even if he survived the impact he would have drowned. 'I was going down very fast. My strategy was to wait until I was a minute from crashing and then cut away one ton of fuel canisters.' It is remarkable his hands were not shaking too violently to make the cut, but this broke the force of the drop to make it 'survivable'.

'The impact knocked me out and I was injured. But it was a happy surprise when I woke up because I don't think anyone had landed that hard in a balloon and survived.' The capsule landed upside down and on fire, so he baled into his life raft and waited 23 hours at sea for rescue. 'I was totally unworried. I just had to wait.'

It didn't put him off and when he did, finally, make it around the world he couldn't stop because the deflation cord broke so the balloon bounced painfully along the ground in the Australian outback for three miles.

By now Fossett's fame was growing but, far from revelling in attention, he showed scant regard for any hullabaloo. 'I've no need for publicity because I'm not trying to make money. I'm doing it for my own interest.'

It is more, not less, remarkable that he is shy, courteous and of average build with thinning grey hair: real action heroes do not look like Arnie. There is no disguising his steely nature, however. 'I thrived in the business world. It really suited my competitive temperament. In the 1980s I spent 100% of my time on work. A few years ago I decided I didn't want to spend any time on it.'

So he sold his companies and threw himself into adventure. He is clearly driven, even obsessive; relaxation is alien. Slippers and pipe seem as far off as ever. 'I'm surprised I'm 59 already; I don't know how I got there. I don't expect to feel limited for at least another decade.'

And how many more records will he break by then?

*The Sunday Times News Review*, 11th April 2004, by Jasper Gerard

See **Checklists!** on page 89 for a list of possible points.

# Practical session 2.3.5

**Spend 15 minutes on this question. The writer of this letter has expressed strong views about genetically modified food. How has his viewpoint been developed?**

**In your answer consider:**

- **the arguments presented**
- **the tone used**
- **the use of paragraphs and variety in sentence structure.**

*Sir*

*I'm sick and tired of all the nonsense that's being spread around about genetically modified food. Just what is the basis for treating GM foods as if they should be regarded as the Devil's concoction?*

*Surely, what we need is clear and sensible information about this new technology and the benefits it could bring to our food supply. Instead, what we have is a great deal of controversy – much of it fuelled by mindless scare-mongering in the tabloid press – about the introduction of GM crops and foods. I would argue that the three GM foods approved for sale in the UK – cheese, tomato paste and soya – are as safe to eat as any other, and I have no hesitation in doing so. Also, 300 million Americans have been eating GM soya for several years now without any ill effects!*

*I recognise that people have concerns. These concerns must be addressed if the future benefits are to be fully realised. Scare-mongering, however, does not contribute constructively to a rational and informative public debate on this important issue.*

*Genetic modification could be the key factor in improving both the quality and quantity of the world's food supplies. In short, it could be used to feed the world. There are 100 million people starving and 800 million people hungry in the world today and the global requirement for food could double in the next two generations. Improvements that could be introduced to crops using GM technology include disease resistance, improved nutritional value and the ability to survive in conditions as barren as the Sahara Desert. A new type of rice with increased vitamin A and iron content is almost ready to meet a huge need in SE Asia, where blindness and anaemia are serious problems.*

*It seems perverse, even criminal, to walk away from such potential when it is needed so desperately. Television images of pot-bellied, starving children could become a thing of the past. How can we, in the West, turn our backs on a cure for world hunger?*

*Many people are concerned that growing GM crops could lead to irreversible harm to the environment. However, since when has conventional farming been a NATURAL process? The crops farmers grow today are very different from their wild ancestors. Yields are artificially increased too. This is due to the use of fertilisers, insecticides, fungicides and herbicides. Current GM technology is aimed at achieving crops, which eliminate the need to spray them with these deadly chemicals that are so harmful to the environment. How could this be an environmental catastrophe?*

*ALL types of farming, including organic, have some negative impact on the environment and new techniques are being developed all the time to minimise the harm caused. Genetic modification should be viewed positively as another option and as part of an overall trend towards greater efficiency and sustainability.*

*Much has been written and said about the perceived risks of GM technology. In fact GM crops have been rigorously tested and offer many benefits to us all. So, what sort of world do we want to live in? I, for one, want a world where we can use new technology safely and constructively. This can only be achieved if we keep our heads and stop this emotional campaign against GM foods.*

*Yours etc*

See **Checklists!** on page 89 for a list of possible points.

# Question 4: A comparison of media and non-fiction

This question is probably the most demanding of the three because it requires you to **compare** the two texts you have so far looked at individually in Questions 2 and 3. However, your task is made slightly easier by the fact that you already know Texts A and B quite well, having commented on each in these first two questions.

Let's look at a typical question 4:

> You must discuss both texts. This can be done in one of two ways. Either write about the first text and then consider the second, remembering to make cross references, or compare the two texts as you work your way through the range of comparisons that you have discovered.

4. Answer using **Text A** and **Text B**. Spend about **15 minutes** on your answer.

   These texts present very different views about how effectively hospital trusts are working.

   **Compare** how the writers have used words and phrases in order to present their viewpoints *or* to make their views convincing *or* to strengthen their viewpoints.

> Remember you are looking at **both** texts!

> Always check your time allowance and then decide how you intend to divide your time between planning and writing your answer.

> The focus of the question is outlined.

# Further advice

To answer this question successfully it is necessary that you:

- identify the writer's **purpose** or **intention** in each text:

  In this advertisement, the writer is trying to promote sales of the new ...

- grasp clearly the writer's **tone** in each text, i.e. his/her particular attitude or approach to the issue being dealt with:

  In this article, the writer has been very disappointed by his experiences and he writes in an outraged tone about ...

- understand how **language devices** are being used by each writer to make his or her views more interesting or convincing:

  The writer of Text A relies heavily on flattering adjectives to make the ... sound appealing while in Text B the writer adopts a more mocking approach, using puns to make fun of it.

- select appropriate **cross references** from the texts to prove or illustrate the differences in the writers' attitudes:

  In Text A we read of 'the thousands of satisfied customers' while the writer of Text B refers to 'a number of disgruntled clients' who contacted him recently.

- make appropriate **comments** on the examples/cross reference you select. Remember that it is not enough to merely state or quote what each writer says. You must show in your comments that you understand and appreciate what the writer is trying to do and how effective he or she is:

  In Text A the writer wants to make his readers very concerned about this health issue and he plays successfully on their anxieties by using expressions such as 'this alarming trend'.

A **wide range of language devices** can be employed by writers to help them make their writing lively, interesting or convincing. For example, writers can make use of:

- specifically chosen **facts or statistics** to reinforce opinion:

  an amazing 96% of ...

- **exaggeration** to emphasise viewpoint:

  this so-called restaurant bore a distinct resemblance to the workhouse kitchen in Oliver Twist

- frequent **questions or exclamations** to challenge or startle the reader:

  Do you really want your children to ...?

- specially chosen **descriptive terms**, to flatter:

  (elegant, spacious, cosy) or to criticise (pathetic, nightmarish, disgusting)

- **superlatives** – words which suggest the product described is the best:

  the very latest, the ultimate in

- **humour**, to make the writing more lively and appealing

- **shock tactics**, using language deliberately designed to frighten:

  a catastrophe waiting to happen

- reference to **expert opinion** to support his case:

  renowned medical expert, Professor Roy Jones, of Great Ormond Street Children's Hospital, says ...

- reference to **satisfied customers**

- **sarcasm**, to mock the subject under discussion

- **comparisons**, especially in the form of similes or metaphors, to enliven the writing:

  *driving the ghastly new ... is like wrestling with an out-of-control World War 1 tank*

- **alliteration** to enhance the appeal of the language:

  *later, visit our own dazzling disco show, where you can swing to the sound of the sixties*

- a **friendly, personal approach** to appeal to the reader:

  *our aim is to ensure that you, our valued customer, can ...*

However, each topic which provides the focus for the question and the texts associated with it will feature widely differing techniques and strategies, so it is best to regularly practise your skills in analysing and comparing writers' methods to increase your confidence for the question you will face in the examination.

# Time to get practical!

On the following pages are two paired texts for consideration. In each case read both texts carefully before allowing yourself 15 minutes to answer the question.

In the first case, **Practical session 2.4.1**, some useful comments and cross references are outlined for you. Try **Practical session 2.4.2** by yourself and compare your responses with the appropriate checklist at the back of the book.

## Practical session 2.4.1

Answer using **Text A** and **Text B**. Spend **15 minutes** on your answer.

These texts present different views about a hotel called Lexington Hall.

**Compare** how the writers have used words and phrases in order to present their viewpoints.

## Text A

A media text that is an advertisement for the hotel

# Lexington Hall
## Five hundred years of hospitality!

Nestling in the rolling hills and lush green valleys of the Cotswolds, the most beautiful landscape in England, is the pride of British hotels, the four-star Lexington Hall. Why not treat yourself and the one you love to a relaxing weekend break or a longer holiday in the unashamed luxury of this award-winning hotel?

This graceful and elegant mansion was first built as a private home in the sixteenth century and it played host to its most famous guest, King Charles, who was sheltered here from Cromwell's victorious troops in 1651.

Extensively and sympathetically restored in 2001, this magnificent manor house has been given a new lease of life, offering the comforts demanded by today's guests while retaining the grace and elegance of a bygone age. Ancient beams and crackling log fires in the sumptuous public rooms create an atmosphere that is both cosy and full of character.

Upstairs, the accommodation is superb and our four-poster beds and gleaming luxury bathrooms are there to indulge you. All bedrooms are individually and handsomely furnished with a blend of bold fabrics, elegant antiques. Most rooms offer pleasant views over our flower-filled formal gardens, with their sweeping lawns, to the beautiful tapestry that is the English countryside beyond.

The centrepiece of the hotel is the lavishly decorated Regency Restaurant, where the service provided by a hand-picked team of attentive staff is impeccable. A wide range of mouth-watering dishes can be selected from our gourmet menu, where the emphasis is on local produce and fresh ingredients.

Why not join the thousands of satisfied guests who have experienced the tranquillity and relaxation of a stay in the splendour of Lexington Hall? For further information, visit us today for a virtual tour of our facilities on our extensive website at www.Lexhall.com

# Text B

A non-fiction text from a book by American travel writer, Ron C. Allworth

## Lousy Lexington!

When I booked my first overnight stay in an English hotel, I suppose I was expecting something special – a hearty, old-fashioned English welcome, a pint of 'real ale' in a cosy bar, a traditional English dinner with roast beef and whatever a Yorkshire pudding is! Perhaps there might even be an old-fashioned English butler who would knock respectfully on my door last thing in the evening to see if I wanted my shoes polished or my trousers pressed.

Unfortunately, it was 'Dream on, Ron!' Indeed, my dream turned out to be a nightmare. I admit that my unfortunate experiences in Lexington Hall were not typical of English hotels generally, but I was certainly greatly disappointed in what was supposed to be a traditional English welcome in a so-called 'hotel of distinction'. Lexington Hall had been recommended to me by a friend who must have had serious problems with virtually all of his faculties, not least eyesight, smell and taste! From the moment I entered the peeling doorway of that crumbling, mouldering ruin, I knew that I would have a most uncomfortable night. How this absolute dump had been awarded four stars was totally beyond me!

The circumstances leading up to my arrival at this hotel from hell were less than ideal. Having sat in my ridiculously small English hire car for four hours on what was allegedly a motorway, in the midst of a ten-mile traffic jam, I spent the next hour or so driving around hopelessly lost, along potholed back-roads in the English rain.

I eventually arrived at the hotel at 8.00 pm, tired and hungry, to be informed that the kitchen staff were going off duty and that it was too late to order a meal. I eventually spoke to a surly, gum-chewing teenager who claimed to be the head waiter, and after much persuasion he agreed to at least offer a snack meal. What he actually dared bring me was something he referred to as an omelette, which had the texture of rubber and the taste of fried trainers.

My room for the night was equally disappointing, a cramped, un-hoovered box, with one small, grimy window offering a splendid view of the sprawling pigsheds of the farm opposite. The faded blue carpet was richly decorated with coffee stains and in the musty bathroom, the bath itself was ancient, cracked and visibly tidemarked. I did not dare investigate the bed too closely! Thankfully, I was so exhausted that I did manage a reasonable night's sleep.

The next day, having survived the breakfast, I paid my bill, registered in detail a number of complaints with the disinterested-looking receptionist and made my escape!

Below are some of the areas that could have been cross-referenced:

☞ The writer's **purpose** in Text A is to present Lexington Hall as a very attractive place to stay, so that lots of tourists will want to come there. Mr Allworth, in Text B, was obviously very disappointed with his stay at Lexington Hall and hence criticises the hotel very harshly. His lively style and savagely humorous descriptions of the hotel, are also aimed at promoting sales of his latest travel book, from which this article is an extract.

☞ The **tone** of Text A is **appealing and alluring** and the reader is promised 'unashamed luxury' in 'the pride of British hotels'. Mr Allworth's tone is **bluntly and savagely hostile**, calling Lexington Hall an 'absolute dump' and describing his relief at being able to 'escape' from it the next day.

☞ **Specially chosen descriptive words** are used by both writers to present, vividly and convincingly, their feelings about the hotel. In Text A, the hotel is lavishly praised in the use of adjectives such as 'graceful' and 'elegant', while in Text B it is said to be 'cramped' and 'grimy'.

☞ The writers also have **very different perspectives of the area** in which the hotel is situated. The 'pleasant views over our flower-filled formal gardens' of Text A contrasts with the reference to the 'sprawling pigsheds' in Text B.

☞ Both writers are **extreme in their attitudes**. In Text A the tone is almost sickly sweet in the metaphor which compares the view of the English countryside to a 'beautiful tapestry', while Ron Allworth totally demeans the place by sarcastically referring to the 'faded blue carpet ... richly decorated with coffee stains'.

☞ They are in stark disagreement also on the subject of the **service at the hotel**. A 'hand-picked team of attentive staff' in Text A hardly matches with the American's encounter with the 'surly, gum-chewing teenager ... head waiter'.

☞ The technique of **using exaggeration for effect** is also employed by both writers, to hilarious effect in Ron Allworth's description of his omelette which 'had the texture of rubber and tasted like fried trainers'. In Text A, exaggeration is seen in the references to the 'sumptuous' public rooms and the 'superb' accommodation.

☞ In Text A, a frequent language strategy is the **use of questions** which invite the reader to sample the delights of Lexington Hall, for example, 'Why not treat yourself to a relaxing weekend break ...?' However, the very different style of Text B features **outraged exclamations** to show his anger and disgust – 'How this absolute dump ... was totally beyond me!'

Now have a go at identifying other cross-references between the texts and making appropriate comments on them. There are lots of others!

## Practical session 2.4.2

Answer using **Text A** and **Text B**. Spend **15 minutes** on your answer. These texts present very different views of a school.

**Compare** how the writers have used words and phrases to reinforce their viewpoints.

See **Checklists!** on page 90 for a list of possible points.

# Text A

A media text – extract from a school publicity brochure

### *Seven good reasons for choosing Chisholm Academy*

➤ **The ideal location.** *Dramatically situated on a hill overlooking the River Tay and the leafy suburbs of Dundee, the school's stylish modern buildings are surrounded by forty acres of carefully tended gardens and recreation grounds.*

➤ **Modern facilities.** *These include a specially-designed suite of music rooms, complete with recording studio, a state-of-the-art Library and thirty spacious, airy classrooms, all re-furbished to provide the very latest in computer technology. Pupils are also privileged to have the use of our recently-constructed Games Hall and Recreation Centre.*

➤ **An exciting curriculum.** *At Chisholm Academy, Scotland's premier educational institution, we pride ourselves on offering a vibrant and challenging curriculum with a wide range of subjects, both academic and vocational. With the increased focus on the international aspect of today's world, special emphasis is placed on modern languages, featuring frequent cultural exchanges with schools in France, Spain and Germany.*

➤ **Teaching by experts.** *Pupils' learning experiences are guided by a team of enthusiastic, caring and highly-qualified teachers, all experts in their own fields, but equally dedicated to the development of each pupil's skills and talents both in the classroom and beyond. Teaching strategies throughout the school are both enlightened and varied.*

➤ **Extra-curricular experience.** *We take pride in enriching our pupils' experiences and developing both their confidence and their talents in a wide range of extra-curricular activities. Pupils are spoilt for choice, whether their interests lie in the sports field (the school has a long tradition of excellence in rugby and rowing), the drama studio or the debating chamber.*

➤ **Examination successes.** *Examination results consistently reflect our pursuit of academic excellence and the school regularly features in the top ten most successful schools in Scotland at GCSE level. Each year at least 95% of our pupils progress to university study and amongst our distinguished past pupils we can boast two internationally-renowned surgeons and no less than three senior members of the current Scottish Parliament.*

➤ **Pastoral care.** *'Chisholm Cares' is our most cherished slogan and regularly updated school policies ensure that all pupils feel valued, respected and safe in our caring environment. Year Heads are specially trained in counselling techniques and the aim of everyone with responsibility within the school community is to enhance every pupil's social skills and self-esteem.*

## Text B

Non-fiction text – an extract from Eileen Murdock's autobiography

### Hardly the happiest days of my life!

Most of us who have been fortunate enough to achieve some success in our lives pay tribute to the importance of our roots in shaping our future destinies. In particular, such people often write in praise of their old school, expressing the feeling that, but for it, they would have been nothing. I am different, in that I achieved my modest degree of success in spite of the dreadful disadvantage of having spent seven years of indescribable boredom at Chisholm School. Perhaps I did gain something there, at least in a negative sense – if I survived the worst that Chisholm could throw at me I could survive anywhere!

When I first had the misfortune to be sent there by my well-meaning but naïve parents, some twenty-five years ago, my first impressions were of a place that was unspeakably dull and grim. The drab, box-like structure of the main building made it look more like a government laboratory for the testing of pharmaceutical products on innocent animals than a place for nurturing tender young minds. From my first day, when I walked through the rusty gates and across the cracked tarmac of the litter-strewn playground, my main aim was to secure my release from that place of torment.

Classes were utterly dull and uninspiring, restricted mainly to English and Maths, and consisted of mind-numbing rituals of spelling tests and the chanting of meaningless equations. Discipline at Chisholm meant rules, rules and more rules and we were punished for the most trivial offences. Whistling in the playground was frowned upon and running up the stairs was an absolute atrocity!

Not once did I receive a word of positive encouragement from the grim-faced robots employed there to act as teachers. Their duty seemed to be to actively discourage self-esteem in the helpless children consigned to their care.

One afternoon a week we were allowed the privilege of Games, which for the boys meant being encouraged by their sadistic coaches to trample each other into the black mud of our one marshy rugby pitch or, for us girls, the dubious thrill of being transported in the school's battered mini-bus to the shabby, council-run hockey pitches where we would endure frost-bitten fingers and bashed legs or ankles before returning to the delight of Chisholm's celebrated cold showers.

I may be too cynical in my memories of those dark days at Chisholm and the school may well have changed now, perhaps since it awarded itself the grand title 'Academy' two or three years ago. I certainly hope so!

The last part of your revision for Paper 2: Section B is a complete section consisting of Foundation and Higher passages and three questions. It is a chance to put together all the skills you've been practising in a realistic one-hour test. The section is laid out exactly as it would appear in the exam. A Higher paper follows a complete Foundation paper. The leaflets are in black and white but you can find colour versions of them at www.hoddernorthernireland.co.uk/english.htm

## Practical session 2.4.3

# FOUNDATION TIER SAMPLE PAPER

## Paper 2: Section B

This section tests **reading** skills.

- Spend about **15 minutes** reading the texts carefully.

- Answer **all three** questions.

---

2. Answer using **Text A**. This is an advertisement from a magazine. Spend **15 minutes** on this question.

   Consider the way in which colour, pictures and layout have been used to promote the Causeway Coast.

   [10 marks]

3. Answer using **Text B**. Spend **15 minutes** on your answer.

   The writer doesn't seem to be convinced about the merits of the Giant's Causeway. How does he develop and sustain his readers' interest in his point of view?

   In your answer consider:

   - the personal nature of his writing style

   - the use of paragraphs and the variety in sentence structure.

   [10 marks]

4. Answer using **Text A** and **Text B**. Spend **15 minutes** on your answer.

   These texts present different views about tourist attractions in North Antrim.
   **Compare** how the writers have used words and phrases in order to present their viewpoints.

   [10 marks]

* See **Checklists!** on page 90 for a list of possible points.

## Text A

From a brochure promoting the Causeway Coast as a place worth visiting

# A Living Legend

As an area of unsurpassed natural beauty, the Causeway Coast & Glens offers a unique fusion of breathtaking scenery and bustling towns; of fascinating heritage and inspiring myth. A timeless landscape where rugged coastline surrounds silent, romantic glens and lush forests, where Saint Patrick once tended his herds on the slopes of Slemish Mountain, where beautiful beaches beckon and where pure rivers wander through unspoilt lowlands and picturesque villages.

The world famous Giant's Causeway, Ireland's top tourist attraction and UNESCO World Heritage site, with its formations of unusual six sided basalt columns and tales of Irish giants as well as the wreck site of the Armada treasure ship 'Girona' makes it a must for every itinerary.

The dramatic Antrim Coast Road is dotted with romantically beautiful stretches of golden sand with European Blue Flag beaches at Ballycastle, Benone, Portrush and Portstewart, and Ireland's longest beach at Magilligan.

Just 45 minutes by boat from Ballycastle is the intriguing, L-shaped Rathlin Island with its 175 different species of birds.

Experience the beautiful landscape whilst engaging in one of the many activities on offer. Miles of fabulous fairways, including the prestigious Royal Portrush, await the golfer at over 30 courses. Whatever your choice – fishing, sailing, diving, horse riding, cycling or walking – it's all here. This is a region packed with something for everyone, filled with history, myth, beauty and song, and a welcome second to none.

## Go on, discover the magic for yourself!

Northern Ireland Tourist Board

EU Programme for Peace and Reconciliation

This publication is supported by the EU Programme for Peace and Reconciliation.

# Text B

This is what a travel writer wrote about re-visiting the Giant's Causeway

The official, roadside sign leading into the Glens of Antrim, tells its reader, with what is dangerously close to boastfulness, that he/she is now entering 'an area of outstanding natural beauty'. Surely this pre-judges the issue for the visitor? It should be up to the tourist to come to this conclusion *after* a visit rather than have this opinion rammed down the throat *before* the place has actually been seen! But back to the matter in hand ...

The arrival of visitors from foreign parts and the need to play the role of tour guide forced me to think seriously about 'glorious' North Antrim. What should I take these people to see in their few days with us? It shouldn't be hard, I thought, we are reputedly nose-to-tail in striking spectacles, picturesque panoramas and shimmering sand – okay, I appreciate that these are all weather-permitting!

Mercifully 'day one' was dry with enough broken cloud to pass for a 'good day' so I swept my guests straight to 'the eighth wonder of the world' – the Giant's Causeway. In case you feel this is a piece of wild exaggeration (which it is), let me, in my defence, point out that this is how the Causeway was commonly described when I was a child.

We were quickly and efficiently whisked down to the famous hexagonal rock formation by an eco-friendly Ulsterbus – it was painted green – presumably to blend the more easily into its surroundings. The tickets for our party of seven stretched for the better part of a metre – less eco-friendly, I felt, although much less likely to be lost!

Having been to the Causeway before, I did not expect to be surprised by it: and I was not. However, what did surprise me was a real sense of something long since forgotten but immediately familiar. It was a sense of disappointment. A feeling of anti-climax.

Thirty years ago I had had to walk the mile and a half to be disappointed by what stood before me. The problem isn't with the curiosity that one experiences upon seeing this regular rock formation in the midst of nature's normal, random offering. Nor is it to do with the basalt columns being gently washed by the sea whilst hundreds of people clamber pointlessly all over this geometric jigsaw. What makes the *Giant's* Causeway such a disappointment is its sheer puniness. If this sounds like an attempt to be fashionably scornful, I can only assure you that it is not my aim. Let me explain, this rock formation is to be found at the junction of two splendid, rocky bays that have as their backdrops sweeping and dramatic vertical cliffs. The setting has such a natural grandeur about it that its scale makes the actual causeway seem quite insignificant.

I concluded, as I had all those years ago, the place was similar to broccoli – no matter how often I'd been told it was good, I still didn't like it. As soon as I could reasonably do so I dragged my visitors away and headed for beautiful, wildly peaceful Fair Head, where, thankfully, there was no eco-friendly bus.

From '0 4 Pete's Sake!' by Peter Kirkpatrick

## Practical session 2.4.4

# HIGHER TIER SAMPLE PAPER

## Paper 2: Section B

This section tests **reading** skills.

- Spend about **15 minutes** reading the texts carefully.

- Answer **all three** questions.

2. Answer using **Text A**. Spend **15 minutes** on your answer.

   The purpose of the leaflet is to encourage older people to be more physically active. How has the writer made use of presentational devices to achieve this?

   In your answer consider the use made of:

   - colour and images

   - headlines, layout, print types and print size.

   [10 marks]

3. Answer using **Text B**. Spend **15 minutes** on your answer.

   The writer doesn't seem to be entirely convinced about his new training programme. How does he develop and sustain his readers' interest?

   In your answer consider:

   - the personal and humorous nature of the diary writing style

   - the use of paragraphs and the variety in sentence structure.

   [10 marks]

4. Answer using **Text A** and **Text B**. Spend **15 minutes** on your answer.

   These texts present different views about fitness for the over-fifties. **Compare** how the writers have used words and phrases in order to present their viewpoints.

   [10 marks]

* See **Checklists!** in the inside back cover for a list of possible points.

**The inner flap**

**The back of the leaflet**

**The front cover**

## Is it right for me?

To benefit your health, activity doesn't need to be vigorous. Moderate activity and beginning gradually is the way to progress.

If you enjoy good health and do not suffer from heart, bone or joint problems or pains in the chest, you can gradually build more activity into your life without consulting your doctor.

However, always check with your GP if you have had an illness, have any worries about your health, or if you have been inactive for a long time. You can improve your health by becoming more active even after a major illness, such as a heart attack, but you will need to do so under your doctor's guidance.

## Local views

"Physical activity has helped me overcome individual inhibitions and lack of confidence."
**Participant in Get Active in the Community Grant scheme, Banbridge**

"Since becoming involved… I have made new friends and I have lost 1½ stone in weight."
**LH, Nifty 50s Club, Portadown**

*get a life ✨ get active*

Designed and produced by:
**Health Promotion Agency for Northern Ireland**
18 Ormeau Avenue, Belfast BT2 8HS
Tel: 028 9031 1611 (Voice/Minicom)
Fax: 028 9031 1711.
www.healthpromotionagency.org.uk

**HPA** Health Promotion Agency

Investing for Health

AGE Concern NORTHERN IRELAND

Photographs reproduced courtesy of the British Heart Foundation.

2/04

# Make the first move!

# Text A

Above is the outer cover of a three-sectioned A4 leaflet. This is followed on the next page by the inner spread of the leaflet.

**The inside spread**

## 30 minutes a day

**Just 30 minutes a day of moderate activity such as brisk walking can make all the difference to your health as you get older.**

If this sounds a lot, try building up gradually. For example, start with a gentle walk or by trying a new activity for just 10 minutes at a time.

The majority of people, whatever their age or condition, can benefit from physical activity. The greatest benefits are gained by inactive people who start to take part in regular physical activity. You will notice the difference as soon as you begin.

Different types of activities can provide different benefits. For example, you could try:
• walking for strength;
• swimming for flexibility;
• t'ai chi for balance;
• dancing for coordination.

You're never too old to feel the benefits of physical activity. In fact, being active can be an important factor in staying healthy and keeping your independence as you get older.

As well as helping your heart and lungs to work efficiently, maintaining a healthy weight and keeping your muscles and bones strong, regular physical activity can:

• help control high blood pressure and diabetes;

• slow down the loss of bone density that can lead to fractures;

• help you maintain your mobility and independence;

• reduce your risk of a serious fall by improving your posture, balance, flexibility and coordination;

• help you cope with everyday tasks;

• reduce stress, help you relax and improve your sleep;

• help you get out and about and make new friends.

## Getting started

**Be more active every day**
Build physical activity into your daily routine. Walk to the shops or put a little extra effort into housework or gardening.

**Gently does it!**
Start any new activity gradually and progress at your own speed. Don't overdo it - you should still be able to hold a conversation while you're exercising.

**Try different things**
Find out what's on near you and choose some activities you enjoy. Vary the activities you do to maintain interest.

**Make it a social event**
Join a class or group, or go with a friend. There are physical activity classes especially tailored for older people – try your local leisure centre or phone 028 9024 5729 to find out about the Actively Ageing Well initiative in your local area.

# Text B

The following passage is from the diary of Joe Osborne. He is facing up to the challenges of middle age ...

*The great fitness drive!*

Well diary, here we are, still alive at the end of Week One of the road to the new, slim, energy-packed me! How was it I hear you ask? I can sum it up in one word – HELL! I have pains where I didn't know I'd muscle. Yes, I know, my kids (why am I calling them 'kids' – they are opinionated, twenty-plus and annoyingly fit) told me to take it gently and I almost did. The problem is, that lurking below this now rather flabby exterior there are still bits and pieces of the competitive animal from thirty years ago. (I know this requires a real imaginative leap on your behalf, diary!)

Monday was my introduction to the over-fifties 'swim-fit' session. The pool was awash with 'ancients' – I almost felt young! What was meant to be a gentle swim quickly turned into a competitive situation – it wasn't my fault – there was this bloke who was clearly in his sixties. He didn't niggle me – at first – but when he glided effortlessly past me for the third time that was it – I had had enough. I stuck doggedly behind him for the next four lengths by which time my lungs felt as if they were on fire and my gammy left shoulder was howling in protest. I crawled out of the pool along with my dented pride and headed for a shower and a re-think. I came to the conclusion I couldn't keep up with him because my goggles were leaking! Make no mistake, I'll be back, when I'm in better shape and he will eat my wash!

Tuesday was a rest day in the carefully planned programme that fitness-freak, number-one son had so thoughtfully drawn up for me. Just as well. The howling shoulder had, by now, locked solid. As a result I spent most of the day inhaling Deep Heat! The shoulder improved but everyone else in the place complained about the strange smell – very amusing!

To be fair Wednesday was slightly better – half an hour's walking. This, I believed, would be a piece of cake – except of course this new regime means that cake isn't on the menu. As I headed off at a brisk pace, I felt confident, this wasn't going to be a problem – and I was right. It was after I'd been walking for about ten minutes when my new, extremely bright trainers caught the attention of one of my neighbours who happened to be passing (why is it that people always turn up just when you don't want them to). An admiring smirk and 'Nice trainers, Joe!' confirmed my earlier instincts about the footwear – I looked ridiculous. The remainder of my 'power-walk' (who thinks up these utterly daft names?) was okay but boring – it all seemed so pointless, after all the car was sitting at home. I could have whizzed round effortlessly in no time ... well, I completed it and received an encouraging phone call that evening from my personal fitness trainer – as number-one son now sees himself!

Thursday was blissfully inactive – if you don't count cutting the front hedge. I don't want you to think I'm negative but gardening is as mind numbing as it is messy.

I was warned upon pain of death to make sure I put on the heart monitor for Friday's exertions. 'Fifteen minutes maximum with your heart rate between 100–110' these were the instructions ringing in my ears. This was going to be better than Wednesday – at least I got to go in the car to the gym! I don't know why I wasn't surprised but things did not get off to the best of starts and I wasn't even out of the changing rooms! None of the thorough instructions I'd been treated to, had mentioned the 'chill factor' of strapping a COLD heart monitor around my chest. This was the worst bit of the whole experience. (I should have mentioned, diary, that today's 'fun' was to take place on one of those rowing machine things.) My embarrassment on this occasion arrived in the form of my extremely young instructor who very thoroughly and very loudly showed me how to use the machine properly – I can only assume he imagined that almost total deafness was an inevitable part of the ageing process. Once he'd finished, the actual rowing was quite easy, although that could just have had something to do with my lack of fitness as my heart rate raced to 110 before I seemed to have done very much – oops!

It's the weekend now and I'm mentally preparing myself for next week's programme. There you have it, diary, do you think I look any fitter? I thought I detected a rather trimmer waist? A slight bulging of the bicep? Maybe not, perhaps this is going to take longer than I thought!!

From 'The Osborne Report' by Joe Osborne

# Checklists!

## Paper 1 Section A

**Remember: You are not expected to have noted all the following points – the markers are very aware of the limited amount of time in which you have to write your answers! Credit will be given for other valid comments not in these checklists!**

### Page 4: Practical session 1.1.2 – possible points

**Example one:**
- the first person narrative – the reader 'sees' the house through the narrator's eyes and 'explores' the house along with the narrator
- the character's reactions to the surroundings as revealed by his internal monologue: 'looked gloomy'/'I didn't feel like laughing'/'a nasty thought'
- descriptive details of the garden create a vivid picture of abandonment: 'broken fence ... jungle of tall weeds'
- the exterior of the house is intimidating: 'walls ... covered in ivy'/'dark empty windows'
- the detailed description of the inside of the house creates a convincing illustration of its physical particulars: 'windows were boarded over'/'big squarish hall'/'great pieces of wallpaper hanging from the walls'
- interior details reinforce the initial impression of a forsaken place and strongly hint of hostily/danger: 'it was very dark'/'floorboards were rotten'/'rickety stairs'/'huge fireplace ... might fall down at any moment'
- the reference to rats adds a note of revulsion to an already distasteful scene, helping to develop a growing sense of unease
- the appeal to the senses further involves the reader in the character's situation: 'a smell like old cupboards'/'a creaking noise'/'closing with a little bang'.

**Example two:**
- the use of direct speech immediately engages the reader's attention
- the evocative image of the two men walking towards the steam train which 'hissed quietly'
- the short sentence summing up the dreadful weather: 'It was a dirty night'
- the description of the 'dim lamps ... shrouded in steam' is slightly sinister
- descriptive details add to the gloomy scene: 'falling rain ... visible in these patches of light'/'The rain belt... showed no sign of lifting'/'those few passengers heading south'
- the contrast between the awful weather and the comfort and welcome of 'The glowing heat from the firebox'
- Jim's desire to be at home 'feet up before the fire' as he contemplates 'the bleak rain-soaked station-yard' – the reader empathises with him.

### Page 5: Practical session 1.1.3 – possible points

**Example one:**
- the setting reflects the thoughts and feelings of the schoolchild: the stress/dread of the situation
- the reader's sympathy is aroused as most people get nervous about exams
- the opening sentence is factual and neutral, informing the reader where the exam took place
- the next sentence also begins factually, describing a wall display of plaster casts
- this sentence ends with a surprise – a 'normal' classroom suddenly becomes somewhere disturbing
- the plaster casts are personified, which makes them sinister: 'utterly silent and utterly threatening'; the repetition of 'utterly' reinforces the impression of the narrator's distress
- the narrator's feelings of complete devastation at the end of the exam are reflected in the exaggerated description of how 'even the air' he/she walked through 'seemed to crumble in ruin'.

### Example two:
- a pleasant mood is established in the opening sentence: 'the lawn was speckled with daisies that were fast asleep'
- this atmosphere is further enhanced by the subtle use of personification: the landscape is 'touched with a delicate, wandering mist'
- the place has a surreal/magical quality reinforced by the use of simile and metaphor: 'the trees looked unreal, like trees in a dream'/'Around the forget-me-nots ... were haloes of water'
- colour assists in creating a charming/delightful image: 'water that glistened like silver'/'smoke rising from the blue mountain in the distance'
- the tranquillity evoked in the short statement: 'It was quiet, it was perfectly still'
- the sense of promise/anticipation in the last sentence: 'It would be a hot day'.

### Page 8: Practical session 1.1.5 – possible points
- the gate is 'hidden behind the yews and laurels' and 'had not been opened for a long while' – the character appears to be alone in an isolated place
- the wood of the gate is described as: 'damp and swollen and slimy with lichen', giving a slightly distasteful impression
- descriptive details add to the sense of a neglected place: 'untrimmed grass'/'overgrown path'
- the character's unease is hinted at in how she pushes her hands 'down into her pockets' and then 'walked cautiously forward'
- the sudden appearance of the pheasant as it 'crashed out of the undergrowth' surprises the reader as well as startling the main character
- her alarm is evident: 'her heart thundering under her ribs, staring round'
- an intimidating silence is emphasised by the writer and the main character clearly feels anxious: 'She stared round, straining her ears for some kind of sound'
- as the atmosphere becomes more threatening, the character's anxiety develops into real panic/fear: 'strangely reluctant to walk any further'/'the hairs on the back of her neck prickling'
- her sudden awareness 'that eyes were watching her from the thicket on her left' introduces an element of menace
- the strong sense of nervous anticipation: 'Holding her breath she turned her head'
- the reader shares the main character's rollercoaster of emotions as she discovers, with relief, that it turns out to be a harmless fox
- this relief quickly turns to tension again as she surveys the somewhat daunting exterior of the house: 'walls covered in ... scarlet Virginia Creeper'/the 'strangely blind aspect' of the shuttered windows
- the feeling that she is being watched returns this time 'from somewhere behind those shutters'.

### Page 9: Practical session 1.1.6 – possible points
- the first person narrative – the reader is spoken to in a blunt/no-nonsense manner throughout
- the narrator 'talks' the reader through 'a typical night' on the streets, involving the reader fully at particularly critical points
- questions are used throughout to sustain the reader's participation in the reality of street-life: 'Settled for the night?'/'What bruises?'/'One o'clock?'/'What's that?'/'Is he still there?'
- discomfort is conveyed in the narrator's choice of words as he chats about picking a place to sleep: 'it's going to be hard and cold'/'a bit cramped'/'half frozen before you even start'
- the reader is shocked at the grim reality of sleeping rough: 'peed on by a drunk, or a dog'/'lager louts'/'you can end up dead'/'guys who like young boys'/'the psycho who'll knife you for your pack'
- short sentences economically convey how fear keeps the narrator awake: 'Footsteps. Voices. Breathing even.'/'Lie still. Quiet. Maybe he won't see you.'

- severe physical pain is communicated in the narrator's direct invitation to the reader to 'try lying on a stone floor' and the list of bruises 'on hips, shoulders, elbows, ankles and knees'
- other unsavoury problems of street-life are referred to, adding to the depressing picture: alcohol and drug abuse and 'not eating properly'
- the simile 'you'll feel like you fell out of a train' dramatically expresses how someone feels after sleeping rough 'six hours a night for six nights'
- the narrator refers to the cold in some detail/the struggle to 'warm up those feet'
- the reader is directly drawn into the struggle to get some sleep: 'You curl up on your side and your hip hurts … You force yourself to lie still … Your pack feels like a rock under your head'
- the references to counting time give the impression of an endless night of discomfort: 'It can't be only one o'clock …?'/'And so it goes on hour after hour'
- the memory of his 'old room at home' and 'little bed' is poignant, evoking the reader's sympathy
- the concluding paragraph conveys the relentless despair of the narrator's situation: 'tomorrow is certain to be every bit as grim as yesterday'.

### Page 16: Practical session 1.2.3 – possible points

- the main feature of this character is her religious mania. She keeps relics of saints in her house and she goes out to preach, seeing herself as 'the handmaid of Christ'
- she is said to be mad. One child, Fatty, describes her bluntly as 'bloody crackers' and there is a reference to her 'huge, green and mad' eyes
- her eccentricity is emphasised by the gossip and rumours about her extreme behaviour – she is supposed to wear vests made of 'nettles and thistles' and to put 'tin tacks in her shoes'
- she is a creature of habit who follows a simple routine and seldom goes far away from her home
- her appearance is ugly and frightening for the children; the hairs growing from 'her long, pointy chin' are suggestive of witches
- note particularly what the writer wants us to think about this highly unusual character. She presents her as a really grotesque person and evokes the reader's disgust through the similes she uses to describe her: 'Her neck was as wrinkled as a dead tortoise'/the hairs on her chin were 'white and wispy as spring onion roots'/Her eyes were 'the colour of boiled goosegogs'
- note also the use of colour in the presentation of her – there is a suggestion of evil in the 'black crucifix' and in the 'black thick-lensed spectacles'
- although she is said to be not a 'dangerous' maniac, a sense of threat is suggested by the reference to the pleats of her skirt being like 'hot blades in the heat'.

### Page 23: Practical session 1.2.6 – possible points

It is important in this answer that you capture *the sister's tone of frustration and exasperation*. She might make comments similar to the following:

- This household wouldn't function without me! Mum disappears with a headache and Dad just gives up. I'm the only one with any sense of responsibility.
- My brother is unbelievably lazy. Each evening he just lies there on our front porch, feeding his ugly little face with potato chips and orange pop, doing absolutely nothing – and Dad lets him!
- Some time ago we all decided on a fair and reasonable allocation of the household chores – but this lazy little creep just shirks all his responsibilities.
- I have the worst job, washing all the pots and pans – but I don't complain. He won't even do the easy bit, just drying them.
- He's so annoying, with his sarcastic comments about evaporation! I'm not stupid. I know what he's up to, and he's not going to make me lose my temper!

- Dad's so hard to get through to! He's no help at all. I'm forever having to insist that he exercise some discipline over his layabout son. It's about time that he gave that horrible little squirt just what he deserves.
- I hate my brother's insolence! I can just see it in his eyes! He doesn't always say anything but I just know he's thinking horrible things about me.
- He calls me fat and 'porky' sometimes, but I'm glad I'm not a horrible stick insect like him! At least I can appear in public wearing shorts – he wouldn't dare let the world see his spindly little legs and knock-knees!
- I'm fed up with his talk about the lawn, which he supposedly looks after. I know perfectly well he just uses that as an excuse to avoid doing any real work.
- I've really had enough, Judy! One of these days I'm just going to waltz out of here and leave them to it! Then we'll see how they manage without me!

### Page 26: Practical session 1.3.1 – possible points

*The effect created by the use of the first person narrator:*

- the direct nature of the writing is tied in with the first person narration which creates a very personal feel – 'I am an officer … they have given me my notebooks'
- the matter-of-fact first person narration is reflected in the structure – the second and third sentences are short, abrupt and to-the-point
- the reflective, honest and detached nature of the writer's narrator is such that we are unavoidably drawn to him.

*The dramatic situation that unfolds:*

- in the first two sentences the writer creates a reason for her character to be writing what we are reading
- the striking and intriguing statements in the opening paragraph immediately capture the reader's attention – 'and wait. I am committed to no cause, I love no living person … I have no future except what you can count in hours'
- the startling and interesting nature of the revelations – the narrator supports no cause and has no love for anyone 'living'
- the reader's curiosity is further aroused – how has such a seemingly calm character come to be in a situation where – 'like me, he may be better off dead'
- there is a sense of hostility and 'unfinished business' with Major Glendinning – 'He will never make a man of me now, but I don't suppose he'll lose much sleep over that'
- the padre's visit and the narrator's quiet rejection of whatever comfort he could offer is striking. Such is the honesty of the narrator that we believe him when he expresses his sorrow at upsetting his visitor
- the reader is undoubtedly puzzled by the singing of the nursery rhyme 'How many miles to Babylon?' Its relevance is not clear yet it is obviously significant to the narrator.

*The use made of language:*

- the reader is intrigued by the as yet unexplained 'waiting days'/'when it is all over'
- as the piece develops we are drip-fed seemingly disjointed snippets that we try to patch together – what is 'The fait accompli. On His Majesty's Service'?
- the description of 'the attack' offers a thoughtful and unusual insight into military action from 'an insider'
- 'a thick and evil February rain' presents a rare moment of descriptive detail
- the appropriately dismal association, given the death and destruction to come, of 'the mournful earth'
- the finely balanced elements assembled by the writer – 'quiet unimportant places' compared to 'the centre of the world' and again in 'the heroes and the cowards, the masters and the slaves'.

### Page 29: Practical session 1.3.2 – possible points

*The effectiveness of the writer's descriptions of the settings:*
The story is packed with vivid descriptions that give the reader a real sense of the place, the action and the boy's reactions:

- the opening two sentences immediately present the reader with vivid description: 'THE SUN ... setting, spilling gold light on the low western hills ... small boy walked jauntily along a hoof-printed path that wriggled between the folds of these hills'/'clambered on to the wet-soaked sod of land'
- use of dramatic verbs: 'spilling'/'wriggled'/'radiating'/'rumbling'
- plenty of use of adjectives and adverbs to lend a visual appeal: 'golden-edged clouds'/'a reedy lake'/'an exultant whoop'/'rose up languidly'
- use of metaphors: 'splashed upon the hills in a shower of echoed sound'/'weaving web after web on its calm surface'/'a black vein in their grey sides'
- use of similes: 'like blown snowflakes'/'its body black and solid as stone'/'smooth and green as the sky, with a faint tinge of yellow like the reflected light from a buttercup'
- note how his change in mood is reflected in the description of his surroundings: 'The sun had now set and the cold shiver of evening enveloped him, chilling his body and saddening his mind'.

*The way in which the story is told from the boy's point of view*:
Whilst the story is narrated in the third person ('he' in this case), the writer gives us an intimate insight into Colm's emotions and feelings and this engages our interest:
- his positive frame of mind is highlighted: 'walked jauntily'/'after listening to his echoing shouts of delight he ran'
- his excitement is detailed: 'Colm with dilated eyes eagerly watched'
- his mood changes when he stumbles in the water: '... the boy stood frightened'
- there is a sharp change in his mood from being 'delighted' at having discovered the nest to experiencing a 'vague sadness', having picked up the egg and realising the implications of this action
- his friend Paddy voices his earlier fears about the nest and Colm's day in school stretches out 'interminably'
- once out of school the focus stays firmly on Colm and his quest to discover whether or not the wild duck has returned to the nest.

*The build up of suspense as the story comes to its conclusion*:
The reader is gradually drawn into Colm's world as we share his experiences and recognise the basic decency of the boy whose conscience nags him about his impulsive act of lifting the egg out of the nest:
- our empathy with Colm is such that, when 'his faith wavered' at school, we too long to know whether or not his fears are justified
- the miserable weather outside leads him to imagine the nest, forsaken: 'moving sheets of rain – rain that dribbled down the panes filling his mind with thoughts of the lake creased and chilled by wind; the nest sodden and black with wetness; and the egg cold as a cave stone'
- his 'rushing home' signals his intention to the reader and develops the reader's suspense
- the final paragraph is full of descriptions that capture the boy's urgent desire to know – a desire we share: 'his heart thumping with excitement'/'every muscle tautened'/'Colm's heart hammered wildly'
- we share the boy's delight when he discovers all is well. His mood is lifted in the final sentence – despite the weather: 'He drew in his breath with delight, splashed quickly from the island, and ran off whistling in the rain'.

**Page 32: Practical session 1.3.3 – possible points**
**Question 1:**
- the young boy feels secure in the company of his parents: 'His Mammie was beside him ... His Daddy lay stretched in sleep on the sofa.'/'It was nice to be sitting alone with your Daddy and Mammie'
- there is a sense of a comfortable routine: 'Sunday evening was always quiet'
- the room is warm and snug: 'fire-glow filled the room'/'feeling the heat on your knees'

- Charley is surrounded by familiar things that add to the young boy's sense of security: 'the kettle singing, and ashes falling in the grate ... the fire'
- he is relaxed: 'when your eyes got sticky you could just sit and look at nothing.'
- the fire glow is the repeated background to the sudden arrival of the milkman and his father arising: 'in the fire glow'/'the fire winking on his watch-chain and his face all red and rosy'.

**Question 2:**
- he feels extremely secure in the routine of his cosy Sunday evening
- delighted at going out with his father, at night, 'all other wee boys' would be in their beds – it adds to the excitement of the outing
- very observant – the young boy taking in everything around him on his journey – the snow; the greeting from the milkman; the dark sky; the passing tram, etc.
- he feels completely safe in the company of his father – the small hand securely in father's pocket – the policeman poses no threat
- they discuss Missus Dempsey's shop and he innocently comments: 'that's where I buy when I've pennies'
- his behaviour in chapel is typical of a child: swinging his legs; looking about him at the lights of the passing trams; turning round to look up at the organist; asking after the first hymn if they were off home now; fidgeting and being spoken to by his father, and finally falling asleep
- his determination to remember everything to tell his brothers and sisters suggest what a big event this is for Charley
- he seems unconcerned at being laughed at by his brothers and sisters – he doesn't care – as he gets his favourite cake and 'his Mammie was good'.

**Question 3:**
*The way the events of the story are seen from Charley's point of view*:
- evidence of this in the first paragraph – the sense of security and contentment the child experiences: 'It was nice to be sitting alone with your Daddy and Mammie'
- at the end of the first paragraph the imaginative child day-dreaming as he watches the flames of the fire
- the arrival of the milkman and the close observation of the events and the conversation between his mother and father gives the reader a real sense of Charley watching everything that's going on
- the reader is reminded of the relative size of Charley compared to the adults around him: 'Daddy was very tall standing on the floor ...'
- his mother asks that Charley be taken – and he is thrilled: 'out at night ... and all other wee boys in bed'/'He felt big to be out so late'
- the security he feels as he walks past the policeman – normally a rather scary authority figure – but not in the company of his father who is holding his hand
- his childish annoyance in church at having to re-heat another part of the seat
- the incident with the woman behind as he watched her pray – typical of a child to stare inappropriately.

*The use of words and phrases*:
- the use of the child's terms 'Daddy' and 'Mammie' and their constant repetition throughout
- throughout we have a sense of seeing the world through the eyes of this child: 'when your eyes got sticky'/'steam came from his mouth, too'/'the wheels began to unwind black ribbons on the snow'
- the humour generated by Charley's explanation as to why his father's boots squeak/his characteristically childish impatience when the service has only started: 'Are we going home now, Daddy? ... Well, when are we going home?'
- the wandering thoughts of the child are what we would expect – not just cake, but cake with currants.

*The way the structure has been used to develop a child-like sense in the writing*:

- the very deliberate use of short sentences of similar length to create a sense of the child – in the first paragraph, 4 of the first 5 sentences are less than ten words long
- the dialogue between father and son emphasises the sense of an excited small boy – e.g. the discussion about Missus Dempsey
- in the final sentence the writer really captures the sense of young Charley, as in the midst of a series of jumbled emotions and memories, he sinks into sleep

Credit will be given for any other valid comments not present in this checklist.

### Page 36: Practical session 1.3.4 – possible points
**Question 1:**
- the menagerie (the initial setting for the story) and Jools's emotional state are mentioned in the opening sentence and are tied together in the simile that ends the first paragraph: 'his heart beat on his ribs as if it wanted to be let out of its cage'
- to provide a contrast between the revolting creatures, as Jools sees them, and the 'beauty' that is working with them
- the amazing and frequently revolting qualities of the various creatures are used to engage the reader's interest: for example, the wheeler which 'resembled a large lump of dough' and could 'turn itself into virtually any shape or form, or even, when in the mood, turn itself inside out'
- to make it clear to the reader that this story is not set on Earth: 'the hairy gloop from the planet Perseus'/'the wheeler from the planet Dracena'
- the Inner-Space Menagerie and its inter-planetary collection with the amount of detailed description helps to make the setting believable: 'The squit's green head lay flat on the water ...'/'poor hairy gloops exploded if the pressure dropped below a certain number'
- the setting of the menagerie is important in that the two characters we are introduced to both react so differently towards the place and its inhabitants.

**Question 2:**
- dogged – he has been at the Inner-Space Menagerie 'often' to observe 'his beauty among the beasts'
- perhaps a little naïve as his assessment of the girl is based only on her appearance: 'Jools wondered ... this wonderful person – who had such shape, intelligence and style'
- not terribly forward because this is the first time he has spoken to his 'love'
- prepared to act as if he is interested in the wheeler to strike up a conversation
- clearly infatuated: 'He wanted to tell her that she, too, was one of the miracles of the universe'/'he could feel himself melting'
- perceptive and honest enough to recognise his mother is a snob as is made clear from her instructions about not calling their home a cave
- a typical teenager with their usual habits – doesn't go on holidays with rest of family: 'Jools had opted to stay at home, get up late, miss lectures, and write poetry of all things about Whatsername'
- determined to press on with his pursuit of 'Whatsername' despite a less than impressive initial conversation
- resourceful enough to enlist the help of his 'shadowy' uncle
- handles his uncle tactfully
- despite the heroic actions in his dreams, he wakes 'in a sweat, quivering with fear'.

**Question 3:**
*The way in which the story is told from Jools's point of view:*
- Jools's problem, which is stated in the opening sentence (note that it is a statement), immediately involves the reader and catches our attention: 'How Jools Anton P'ntarr loved that girl from the Inner-Space Menagerie!'
- the narrator chooses to tell the story in the third person, but all the thoughts and feelings the reader learns about are those of Jools, who from the opening of the story and the title, appears to be the central figure

- Jools's less-than-successful first contact with the object of his dreams is caught in an immediate way for the reader: 'Nuts, nuts and more nuts to the whooping primates of Cedonia, thought Jools'
- the narrator uses Jools as a means of delivering more of the background to the story – about where he lives, his home and his parents.

*The humour in the story:*
- the contrast between Jools's thoughts and his comments amuses the reader: 'Oh beating heart be still! He spoke his first words to her. "That's a very fine wheeler you've got there"'
- the amusing contrast between the revolting creatures and the beautiful girl – the wheeler called Dot and the girl both described as one of the 'miracles of the universe'
- the conversation hitting 'an asteroid' seems appropriate in a science fiction story
- the reader empathises with Jools's infatuation and is amused by it, as can be seen in this exaggerated description of her eyes: 'two of nature's most perfect gems, both illuminated from within by her natural radiance ...' the reader is equally amused by the effect they have on him: 'and he could feel himself melting. Oh bubbling blood, let him not get carried away ...'
- entertaining contrast between Jools's romantic ideas and 'Pass me that bucket of liver'
- his jealousy and rather awkward efforts do amuse as well as developing our sympathy and interest: 'uncharitable and even nasty thoughts about Bunny Goldman ... called after her rather desperately'.

*The use of words and phrases:*
- the unusual names are noticeable from the early stages of the story: 'Jools Anton P'ntarr'/'Perishing squits'/'hairy gloops'/'the whooping primates of Cedonia'
- 'You definitely are missing a chromosome' is an updated version of a current expression in regular use
- the idea of Jools's parents holidaying on 'Ithica Three', where they are promised 'Stunning volcanic sunsets by the light of *two* moons', sustains the reader's interest
- we are further intrigued by references to 'the visiphone ... this person's Central Registration Number but not the Personal Identity Code. I can't make the call without a PIC.'/'her CRN'.

Credit will be given for any other valid comments not present in this checklist.

## Paper 1 Section B

**The following points are non-specific. They are a general listing of the characteristics and qualities that the examiner will be looking for in this type of answer. As always, credit will be given for other positive features not referred to in this checklist.**

### Pages 42 and 43: Practical sessions 1.4.1, 1.4.2 and 1.4.3 – possible points
- appropriate and convincing development to sustain the reader's interest
- evidence of the ability to analyse, review and comment
- a rounded consideration of all sides of the given issue
- a clear awareness of audience sustained throughout the writing
- appropriate tone throughout
- a clear sense of organisation
- use of appropriate paragraph openings
- control of the conventions of written English
- clear personal engagement with the task and confident, appropriate expression
- a suitable opening paragraph
- a range of vocabulary
- use of language devices such as rhetorical questions
- use of an appropriate vocabulary
- a lively style – use of humour if appropriate
- a suitable conclusion.

Paper 2 Section A

**The following points are non-specific. They are a general listing of the characteristics and qualities that the examiner will be looking for in this type of answer. As always, credit will be given for other positive features not referred to in this checklist.**

**Pages 46 and 47: Practical sessions 2.1.1, 2.1.2, 2.1.3 and 2.1.4 – possible points**

- appropriate and convincing development of the given form of writing
- a sustained and clear awareness of audience
- clear personal engagement with the task
- evidence of the ability to inform, explain and describe appropriately
- development that sustains the reader's interest
- appropriate tone throughout
- use of appropriate language
- a range of vocabulary
- a suitable opening paragraph
- a clear sense of organisation
- use of appropriate paragraph openings
- control of the conventions of written English
- a lively style – use of humour if appropriate
- a suitable conclusion.

Paper 2 Section B

**Page 52: Practical session 2.2.2 – possible points**

- the disturbing, nightmarish image on the front cover sets the tone for the leaflet - it reinforces the idea of the distorting effect of drugs
- the close-up image of the wide open eye, in red, behind the main image further develops the sense of tension that the leaflet is seeking to create
- the inner flap features a face with a glib, naïve comment blocking out the eyes – again this is both worrying and somewhat disturbing
- a further image in red, perhaps as a warning, across the back cover, shows someone abusing drugs
- a range of stray, unsettling images – a face, hands and eyes – are used in the inside spread
- the layout is chaotic – deliberately reflecting the effect of drugs – text is used at odd angles, it is occasionally blurred and meaningless lines and 'doodles' all add to this effect
- black and red are used on a white background to increase the haphazard and random feel of the leaflet
- the sense of a chaotic environment is significantly developed through the use of many fonts; the mixing of upper and lower case lettering, and wildly varying print sizes and styles – these also are visually stimulating and sustain the reader's interest
- the telephone help-line number in large blurred figures – whilst still being perfectly legible – is eye-catching as well as continuing the theme of the distorting effect of drugs
- headings and sub-headings are used in a secondary fashion – they are most in evidence on the inner flap where they still further add to the discordant feel of the leaflet.

**Page 54: Practical session 2.2.3 – possible points**

- eye-catching use of colour in the title of the article: 'ALL CREATURES ...' that leads the reader's eye across to the colourful pictures on the other side of the double-page spread
- all the pictures reinforce the thread of the text as highlights of the holiday: their boat with beautiful surroundings in the background; the B&W image of Gerald Durrell whose writings had led the family to Corfu; the two pictures devoted to the wildlife
- the pictures of the children add personal interest. There is a sense of 'family snaps' that brings with them a sense of empathy and realism
- the layout is unusual as the title is not conventionally located at the beginning of the piece - it is used here to connect the story and the images

- the 'strap-line' also helps to connect the two page spread.

**Page 64: Practical session 2.3.3 – possible points**

- the vivid descriptions built up through the plentiful use of adjectives: 'stunted olives'/'wave-wrinkled sand'/'thick, brown, carunculated [ribbed] leather'
- vividness generated by similes: 'like a carpet of white velvet'/'like a fish's tail'
- the precise idyllic descriptions of the bay and its clear water: 'the bay looked so still and transparent ...'/'through six feet of clear water you could see rocks on which anemones lifted frail, coloured arms'
- his striking and original descriptions of the underwater world: 'we hung like hawks suspended in air above a strange woodland'
- his descriptions appeal directly/immediately to our senses: 'Around my legs the coloured fish flicked and trembled, and stood on their heads while they mumbled at me with toothless gums'
- the amusing anecdote about the sea-slug water pistols
- the final image of the fisherman that brings the excerpt to a suitably tranquil conclusion.

**Page 66: Practical session 2.3.4 – possible points**

*The positive picture created of Steve Fossett's life:*
- tone of admiration throughout – the writer conveys his respect for SF and his achievements
- the writer approvingly contrasts SF with others nearing pensionable age: 'shuffling along to collect their free bus-passes'
- the quotation from Sir Richard Branson – himself a famous adventurer – is suitably flattering
- factual details about his amazing records/achievements are detailed for the reader to appreciate
- even in his leisure activities SF's courage and daring are highlighted: car and husky racing
- the lighthearted references to the traditional view of spending retirement in 'slippers' – help to reinforce the view of SF as energetic/full-of-life
- the writer's compliments throughout: 'His passion began ...'/'It didn't put him off ...'/'It is more, not less remarkable ...'
- the story of SF's remarkable escape in 1998 conveys his endurance/stamina
- the impression given of his former life as a business-man is also one of determination and zeal.

*The sentence structure and use of paragraphing:*
- the opening paragraph summarising some of SF's achievements and ending with an apt quotation from Sir Richard Branson effectively arouse the reader's curiosity
- rhetorical questions as the linking sentences from the second paragraph further draw the reader in
- the sequence of selected biographical details in the next few paragraphs build up a fascinating impression of a brave adventurer
- the use of SF's own words as a first hand account of his highly dramatic survival is absorbing
- this first-person narrative involves the reader directly in the situation and helps convey a sense of the drama/excitement of SF's near-death experience
- much of the piece is structured with quotations from SF interspersed with comments and opinions from the writer which help sensationalise events/highlight his achievements
- the sequence of details about SF's life sustains interest and helps the reader get to know him
- use of a lively style – the reader is caught up by the writer's evident delight in SF's achievements
- the rhetorical question at the end effectively concludes the piece in its direct appeal to the reader.

**Page 67: Practical session 2.3.5 – possible points**

*The arguments presented:*
- the writer presents a series of logical arguments: too much scare-mongering; GM foods are as safe as any other foods;

GM foods could be the answer to a potential food shortage/feeding the hungry; refers to the improvements that could be made using GM technology; addresses environmental concerns – conventional farming techniques not natural/GM crops are less harmful to the environment as the aim is to eliminate need to spray crops with chemicals/even organic farming has some negative impact on environment; GM crops have been rigorously tested

- some of these arguments are well supported with facts and figures – this helps to reinforce the points being made
- some arguments are backed up with forcefully expressed opinions/statements: 'I have no hesitation in doing so'/'This can only be achieved …'.

*The tone used*:
- the opening is very blunt in tone: 'I'm sick and tired …'
- the sincere tone adopted in 'I recognise that people have concerns' suggests the writer is being balanced and rational which helps ensure his audience listen to his viewpoint
- the use of capitals and exclamation marks at particular points further reinforce the forthright tone of the piece
- the confident tone employed by the writer emphasises his no-nonsense/decisive approach to the issue
- the plea at the end of the letter is heartfelt in tone and comes across as sincere/genuine.

*The use of paragraphs and variety in sentence structure*:
- the short opening paragraph effectively conveys the strength of the writer's feelings
- paragraphs 2 and 3 convey the message that he is being fair and sensible in calling for a proper debate without scare tactics
- the writer goes on to offer his arguments for GM foods building up a convincing case/line of reasoning for his viewpoint
- the concluding paragraph directly addresses the reader to share the writer's insight
- the use of rhetorical questions throughout conveys a strong sense of the writer's feelings of dismay and annoyance
- a feature of the sentence construction in this piece would be the use of emphatic statements which add force and energy to his opinions.

### Page 74: Practical session 2.4.2 – possible points

- Text A is an extract from a school prospectus, therefore the writer's purpose is to promote the school in order to attract lots of pupils. In Text B, an extract from an autobiography, the author reminisces about her unpleasant experiences as a pupil in the school. The viewpoints are therefore completely opposed
- the tone of Text A is flattering, presenting the school as 'Scotland's premier educational institution', while in Text B the writer's tone is bitterly scathing – she hated it
- both writers have chosen succinct and eye-catching titles, each one making use of alliteration to make the writing more appealing – 'choosing Chisholm' and 'Hardly the happiest'
- the writers have opposing viewpoints on the school's appearance – Text A praises the 'stylish modern buildings' while Text B tells of the 'drab, box-like structure of the main building'. In Text B, Eileen Murdock underlines her hatred of it by comparing it to a 'government laboratory for the testing of pharmaceutical products on innocent animals'. This unpleasant comparison is followed up in her remark a few lines later that Chisholm was for her a 'place of torment'
- in Text A, the description of the school grounds is very appealing – 'forty acres of carefully-tended gardens and recreation grounds'. However, Text B presents a very different picture with the mention of 'rusty gates', 'cracked tarmac' and 'litter-strewn playground'
- Text A makes use of a small number of facts and statistics to enhance the image of the school: the grounds extend to forty acres, some of the facilities are listed, and the claim that '95%' of students went on to university. Text B is almost entirely personal opinion and where facts are mentioned

they are often coloured by negative descriptions – the sports coaches were 'sadistic'
- the most striking contrast is in the writers' opinions of the quality of the teaching at Chisholm. Text A claims that teachers are 'enthusiastic, caring and highly qualified' and their teaching methods are 'enlightened and varied'. Eileen Murdock shows her cynical viewpoint again by calling the teachers 'grim-faced robots' and their classes 'utterly dull and uninspiring'.

Credit will be given for any other valid comments not present in this checklist.

### Page 77: Practical session 2.4.3 – possible points
**Question 2**:
- the main image is a stunning picture of the region which is both idyllic and extremely attractive – it is striking and is being deliberately used to catch the attention of the reader
- the smaller image of the Causeway itself features the rock formation – it is used to develop the reader's interest as well as showing the 'attraction' on a bright, sunlit day
- a couple of logos are featured at the bottom of the advertisement; they have the effect of giving the content a feeling of official status and a sense of approval or authenticity
- the shape of the N. Ireland Tourist Board logo reflects the causeway columns
- the heading, in vivid blue, effectively connects the twilight image with the text – the slightly mysterious feel of the picture ties in well with the notion of 'legends'
- the coloured strap-line with its size and exclamation mark enthusiastically urges the reader into action
- the layout of the text is 'user-friendly' because it has been clearly broken up into a series of short paragraphs that make it an easier and more inviting read.

**Question 3**:
- the piece opens with an opinion that aims to catch the reader's attention: 'The official, roadside sign … is dangerously close to boastfulness … Surely this pre-judges the issue … ?'
- he uses an engaging conversational style to draw in his reader: 'It shouldn't be hard, I thought'/'okay, I appreciate that these are all weather-permitting!'
- the writer shares his problem with his readers in order to engage us: 'the need to play the role of tour guide forced me think seriously about "glorious" North Antrim'
- we are drawn in by the first person narration: 'Thirty years ago I had had to walk'
- his unusual way of observing what he sees: 'we are reputedly nose-to-tail in striking spectacles, picturesque panoramas and shimmering sand'/the description of the bus tickets
- the slightly cynical feel: 'an eco-friendly Ulsterbus – it was painted green'/'hundreds of people clamber pointlessly'
- the conversational tone is often reflected in the sentence structure: 'I did not expect to be surprised by it: and I was not'
- the sentence structure is occasionally quite complex: 'In case you feel this is a piece of wild exaggeration (which it is), let me, in my defence, point out … when I was a child'
- the writer uses short, abrupt sentences for emphasis: 'It was a sense of disappointment. A feeling of anti-climax'
- the paragraphing is initially used to help develop the conversational style: most obviously with the second, one-line paragraph
- the writer uses the paragraphing to differentiate between his experiences in the present and those he remembers from thirty years ago.

⬤**Question 4**:
- Text A is uncritical in its praise of the area whereas Text B is more guarded and selective in its praise
- the opening paragraph of Text A is a breathless series of positive, opinion-packed lists: 'a unique fusion of breathtaking scenery and bustling towns; of fascinating heritage and inspiring myth'